MANY WERE CALLED–
FEW WERE CHOSEN

The Story of Mother Earth
and
the Earth-Based Volunteers

Dr. Heather Anne Harder

ISBN 1-884410-00-6

Published by

Light Publishing
210 So. Main St., Suite 203
Crown Point, IN 46307
(219) 662-7248

a division of

The Association of Universal Light Volunteers
210 So. Main St., Suite 202
Crown Point, IN 46307
(219) 662-7074

Printed in the United States of America

Cover Art: NASA Photo S31-83-90

Illustrations created by Diane Rae (Carnahan)
Footnote illumination by Michael Tyree
Cover design by Michael Adam

ACKNOWLEDGMENTS

My sincere appreciation to my dear friends and family who have assisted with the preparation of this manuscript. Their kindness and support helped make the hours pass more quickly. Their willingness to edit and review the material helped to provide insight and clarification to the big picture. There were many who assisted and all are loved.

A special thanks to Charles David Heineke, Deborah McGrew, Brian Kuss, and Doris Bishop, for their technical skills and intellectual inspirations; to Diane Carnahan, for her artistic insights, and to Willie Culberson, for his faith and willingness to serve Mother Earth. My thanks also to Bob, Kerri, and Stacie, my dear family, who have ever been a mirror for my many lessons; and finally, to my father and deceased mother, who have taught me to stand tall in the face of adversity and to respect the truths of others, even when they are not my truths.

To these and the many more unnamed friends in all dimensions of existence, I offer my gratitude.

Table of Contents

A Word About the Author, Dr. Heather Anne Harder

A Letter From Heather

A Campaign for the Presidency

Campaign "Chain Letter"

If You Would Like to Help...

Introducing... The Association of Universal Light Workers (AULV)

AULV Membership Form

Books By Dr. Heather Anne Harder

Chapter One

In the Beginning There Was Choice

n the beginning, God created the Heavens and the Earth, and they were good. God called the Earth *Terra*, and it was to be unique in all the universe. Terra would allow free will to reign. Free will was, in itself, a unique challenge. When planets had been formed in the past,[1] they had always been designed to test or develop one or two aspects of a being. Planets, which allowed for the exploration and growth in the areas of emotions, fluidity/flexibility, or perhaps perception, were relatively easy to accomplish, but giving total free will was truly unique. Unlimited choices also meant that there had to be a way of allowing those unlimited choices and of allowing beings to live with the unlimited consequences of those unlimited choices. This was a logistical nightmare, even for the Divine God Source.

Terra was to be a place where each being's experiences, and life would be a unique expression of the individuality of the person. The life experienced would be the result of the individual choices made. This was an enormous endeavor.

The God Essence gave free will to Earth, and it was truly a wondrous gift. Free will was to be the Divine plan for Earth. This plan provided for even the smallest detail. And this was good, as the Divine plan always is.

Free will did not come easily. Free will meant that humanity had to choose from a variety of alternatives. Choice had to be extended into every domain imaginable, both physical and nonphysical. Therefore, alternatives had to be created in every arena. Unlike all other planetary existence, Terra had to provide unlimited choice in every domain. There had to be infinite variety in such things as food choice, plant life, weather conditions, living arrangements, skin colors, and hair textures. From the smallest detail—blades of grass or snow-flakes, to the largest creations—the beasts that roamed the Earth, there was a boundless variety. This would give those of Earth the opportunity to truly choose. Thus, in the beginning, God provided for all choice.

To ensure that free will would be the law of the land, Earth-eans were allowed to maintain the ability to co-create with the God Essence. The ability to co-create is always possible *outside* the laws of physical, but to maintain this ability *while in physical* was somewhat new. Yet this ability to co-create allowed those of Earth the ability to give birth to an even more unique world and provided an even greater ability to choose, and then live with, those choices.

[1] *New worlds must be constantly evolved to ensure classroom space for those that need it. New worlds replace the old ones that no longer serve their intended purpose and those that provide lessons which are no longer needed, just as new schools are built to replace old ones on Earth. Each new planet is different; it can never be just the same as the old one or serve the same function. Therefore, unlike the tearing down of the old schools, old planets are never discarded. Instead, more choices are provided and new opportunities for growth are ensured.*

Humanity was given the ability to co-create with God because humanity can never create in the *absence* of God. This God/creator power gave humanity the ability to be the creator of an ever-new and changing world of their own design. God's plan for Earth was free will. This Divine plan allowed each human the right and the responsibility to create their destiny. If it was created in harmony with God, then all was created from love; if not, then humanity had the opportunity to experience that and then choose again. This was the Divine plan for Earth. And this was good, as the Divine plan always is.

Divine plan gave Terra the uniqueness of being a dynamic, ever-changing world, a world in which those in residence would determine its path. Each individual was given the ability to contemplate his/her own reality. In this ability to contemplate was seeded the Creator's ability to create. The Divine plan allowed for each person to both perceive and create with *mere thought*. This was the only way to allow for the diversity of choice needed on the planet. And this was good, as the Divine plan always is.

Choice mandated that alternatives had to be present. As beauty and light were present, so, too, were the various shades of darkness.* Thus, darkness, too, was part of the Divine plan, for if people did not experience darkness, then how could they truly know the light with full awareness? Darkness was never meant to be judged, only experienced. The forces of light and the forces of darkness were always kept in balance so that free will could prevail. In the beginning, balance was important, just as it is now. It is through balance that humanity is able to freely choose without outside pressure and influence. And this was good, as the Divine plan always is.

Terra was given specific cycles to ensure that new experiences or choices would always be present on Earth. Cycles were put into place that allowed for all things, including growth and weather patterns, as well as planetary influence. These cycles were determined by the Creator in the beginning. Thus, these cycles could not, would not, and will not be changed, except by Divine intervention. The Divine plan had proven to be perfect. And this was good, as the Divine plan always is.

The first Earth inhabitants in human form were much different than we know today. We would probably label them more as spirits, as they possessed only a light body and were not physically limited nor bound by a permanent physical body. They had the ability to move in or out of physicality and assume any form. They could easily choose to be in a physical embodiment as we know it, or they could choose total freedom from it.

Moving in and out of any physical form desired allowed them to experience the state of consciousness of that form for as long or as short a time as they wished. They could experience a tiger stalking its prey and instantly experience being the prey. They could experience the solidity of a rock and the nobility of a tree, with the flicker of a thought. This gave them compassion and a deeper understanding for what existence was like for all life forms on Earth.

Best of all, those early inhabitants were always very connected to the Divine consciousness. They were never separated from the God Force that had created them. Their vibrational life force was in perfect

> ** Words marked by this symbol are often used elsewhere as judgmental terms and perhaps may even carry a negative meaning. This is not meant here, for all things are but experiences. Thus, these words as used here denote no greater or lesser value or "goodness." Unfortunately, there are no judgment-free words available that express the desired meaning. Therefore, these words will have to do.*

harmony with the vibrational life force of the God Source. This connection was the reason they could instantly manifest into any and all physical forms. They shared the creative nature with God. God is both the creation and creator. Therefore, humanity shared the ability to be both the creation and the creator. Eartheans recognized that they could experience physical life from many perspectives and learn from each, but they never confused themselves—their Divine Essence—with their physical form creation.

Life was abundantly filled with unconditional love; so whatever choice was made—even darkness, for that, too, was a choice—life was always filled with joy, peace, and harmony with the Creator and all creation. Earth existence was a playground of experiences, a virtual Disneyland of delight. The Divine Intelligence had provided all that was needed for a life of abundance. The Divine Intelligence had provided all that was needed for a life filled with unlimited joy and love. All Eartheans had to do was choose it. And this was good, as the Divine plan always is.

Eartheans could move into other dimensions and worlds with ease, as it was their own desire, held in thought, which moved them. The consequences of their thoughts were immediately realized and the process was fully understood. Those of Earth realized the wisdom of the Divine plan. They maximized their use of the power that was given them. There was great happiness, the magnitude unlike anything that could be imagined today. If a choice was made that brought an unpleasant* consequence, then they merely altered the choice. There was no guilt or self-recrimination, for they realized that *they and only they* had the ability to alter or control their own destiny. No reactions such as blame, guilt, anger, or aggression were needed or felt. They would merely correct their path, right the error,* and move on, secure in the knowledge of their relationship with the God Force and the wisdom of the Divine plan. The love and the joy experienced during this time knew no bounds. Free will provided the opportunity to explore and to grow through this process of exploration and experience. These physical form experiences provided unique opportunities for awareness and growth. Eartheans knew it and appreciated the great gift of physicality. And this was good, as the Divine plan always is.

Life in this fashion went on for eons of time, as the cycle of life, death, and rebirth had not yet been created, for it was not yet needed. Humanity, in its role of co-creator with the God Force, had played, explored, and created many exotic forms.

The animal kingdom offered many opportunities. Some Eartheans had assembled the head of one beast, the tail of another, and the skin of another, much as children of today play "what if"—"What if a giraffe had wings?" and so forth. But when the earlier Earth inhabitants played this game, these strange creatures were brought into existence. The Eartheans did not always see the need to reinstate the original form; after all, God had given them dominion over the beasts. Those playing this game often liked the many new forms created, even though they were not always the most pleasant, comfortable, or convenient for the beast.

This was the beginning of the first problem that humanity created for itself. Eartheans had begun to become more concerned with self's desires than with the welfare of the beasts and others in their care. This caused a vibrational² change. For the first time, Eartheans had lowered their Divine vibration, causing them not to resonate in Divine harmony with the God Force. It had been their choice—they were fully aware of that—but because of their own choice, for the first time Eartheans were not fully connected to the universal consciousness. They were no longer an equal part of the God Force, and this non-connection caused them great despair. Eartheans were still potentially and theoretically equal, as they are now. They were a spark of the pure God Divine Source. Their essence was the Essence of God. They knew it and yet had made choices that had altered their divinity. Then, as now, they were fully creating what they experienced and fully experiencing what they had created. They had chosen, at least temporarily, a path of pain and separation from the God Force. They knew it and assumed full responsibility for it.

The process is much like listening to a radio while traveling in a car. As you travel farther from the radio station, the static increases and it is harder to understand. If you adjust your dial, you can often get the station more clearly. Each mile you travel causes the reception to fade. At some point you must decide whether the trip or the radio transmission is more important. If the trip is of greater value, you proceed and find another station or turn off the radio. If the transmission is more important, you must turn around and head back the way you came. When Eartheans resonated to the same frequency as the God Force, the reception was clear; God's thoughts were the thoughts of humanity. But as the Eartheans began to lower their frequency, the connection between God and them became less clear. When in harmony with God's vibrational frequency, all of humanity resonated with unconditional love and light; but as the connection faded, so did this state of bliss. Eartheans had to choose to travel back to the frequency of the Divine connection or travel on without it.

> [2] *Every creation has a molecular movement of the atomic structure. This is an energy movement and is known as the vibrational frequency. Humanity had resonated at the Divine frequency; therefore it was "at-one-ment" with the Creator. With this connection, humanity had access to all knowledge and truth. As humanity made choices that caused the lowering, or slowing, of this vibrational frequency, it lost the ability to be at one with God. This came to be known as the descent of humanity. Currently, Eartheans are reawakening to the process needed to raise their vibrational frequency so they will once again experience the unconditional love and joy that is always present in the Divine frequency. This can happen easiest when they realize that love is the answer. More on this later.*

As this process occurred in the Earthean experience, many chose to reconnect to the God Source, and others chose to continue the trip in a state of separation. Thus, humanity continued on their physical journey. This decision was (and is) an individual one and can be made at any time, for each must decide which is worth more, the connection to the God Essence or the life of illusion and separation.

The second major problem developed when others who had remained in harmony with, or had chosen to reconnect with, the Divine Force, began to "help" those who did not maintain that harmony. In some instances, they insisted that their way be followed because, after all, they knew what was "best." This was the problem...*judgment*!

First, Earth was and is a free will planet. *Divine plan mandated that each be allowed to follow her/his own choice, with no exceptions.* It was imperative that each follow his/her (there was no gender orientation at that time) own guidance and free will. One was *never* to infringe on the free will of another. Yet here were well-meaning humans trying to influence and even mandate the behavior of another because they had first judged the other's choice to be inferior or wrong. Even though the gesture was well meant, the judgments and the resulting interference caused major alterations in the vibrational nature of humanity and they continue to do so on this planet.

Had humanity honored and respected each individual's right to free will, Earth and humanity would be in a very different place today. Then (as now) humanity forgot that there are no right or wrong choices, only alternatives which bring about different consequences, for always humanity is responsible for their choices.

Judgments of others caused major alterations in the divine frequency. The more humanity judged one another, the more they fell from the grace of the Creator Source. The more humanity judged one another, the more they taught judgments to each other. Judgments be-got more judgments. They could have shared their insights with each other with unconditional love and unconditional respect for the choices of others, but they didn't; they judged, and that was the second major frequency disturbance on beloved planet Earth. Humanity was free to choose and they chose to judge.

As a consequence of those judgments, humanity tried to control and manipulate the behavior of their fellow humans. If only those well-meaning ancestors had simply shared the array of choices rather than trying to dictate the right behavior, life would be very different today. But they didn't; instead, they held onto the outcome. They tried to force their choice on others. They were thus in violation of Divine law and they greatly disturbed the Divine frequency.

As a result, a new cycle was put into place on Mother Earth—that of judgment/manipulation/control. It was, and is, one of the single most destructive choices which humanity has created, for it violates the heart of the Divine plan. It goes against the will of God. God allowed for *all* choice and had created a process for one to experience the consequences of those choices, but humanity had defied it. Thus, this was the knife that created total separation from God. Humanity had willingly cut themselves off from the oneness of all creation. Yet this, too, was allowed, under the laws of Divine plan. And this was good, as the Divine plan always is.

As Eartheans took their eyes off their own path in order to examine the paths of others, they began to lose sight of the game which they were playing. They began to take the whole process *seriously* and forgot to *enjoy* it. *This lack of joy and the introduction of judgments greatly reduced the Eartheans' vibrational frequency.*

With the introduction of judgments, some Eartheans began to feel superior or inferior to others, depending on the outcome of their judgments. They forgot that all are equal and that all choices bring lessons and growth, and that none are better or worse than others. Diversity of choice was planned for and allowed in Divine law. These feelings of inferiority and superiority were also in disharmony with the God Force vibration.

Eartheans were now on a sled, moving, at first imperceptibly, down a great vibrational hill. This was their choice. The God Force allowed it to be. They still had knowledge of the Divine plan and maintained a full awareness that all they had to do was create a new experience. Yet their choices only served to continually lower their God Force vibration. This, again, was their choice, and was allowed, according to the Divine plan.

The vibrational shift occurred slowly at first. As eons of time elapsed, the vibrations were considerably lowered. The vibrational center of humanity is in the heart area; therefore, these changes have often been referred to as changes in the hearts of Eartheans. These changes resulted in an even greater awareness of the separation from the God Force and the universal consciousness. This caused an even greater despair in humanity, which, in turn, brought about an even greater lowering of the vibration.

Free will was still in operation. Eartheans knew of the love and joy that awaited them in the realms of the higher vibrations. They knew their choices were causing pain instead of pleasure. They knew these were the consequences of Earthean free will. They knew of the wisdom of the Divine plan. This was good, as the Divine plan always is.

Suffering had been introduced to Earth. *It had been created by those in residence.* It had been created because of the fall, or lowering, of the God Force vibration of humanity. It had caused humanity to turn to self-concern rather than to the knowledge that each individual was truly one with the universe. They had forgotten that life was meant to be a game played for sheer joy and experience. Instead, certain choices had been made by those in residence, and they now had to live with the painful consequences of those choices. Humanity could have made choices that resulted in raising its vibrations. It did not. This, too, was their choice.

Slowly at first, but then more rapidly (for time did not yet exist), Eartheans lost many of their wondrous abilities, due to the lowering of their vibrational frequency, which was synonymous with the separation from the God Essence.[3] Eartheans ceased to be able to easily move in and out of physical form. As their individual vibrations lowered, their ability to instantly manifest was also lessened. Their creations took longer to become apparent.

They began to *doubt* their own abilities to co-create with God and, thus, their doubts became their reality. They could no longer travel just by willing it. Some Eartheans got stuck in their unusual created forms.[4] Others had simply hardened into one form or another. Much of the unbridled pleasure once known to them had been lost. Their choices had greatly limited their subsequent choices, though they still had the right to choose and to change their choice. They still had the right to expand or diminish their choices, and they knew it; yet change they did not. Eartheans continued to behave in a way that served to further lessen their choices.

God had given them the choice, the ability, and the right to choose, for, indeed, this was the law of free will. And this was good, as the Divine plan always is.

[3] *The Creator planned for all eventualities through a safety factor built into the Divine plan. The more attuned one is to the universal God Essence, the more ability one has to co-create. The further one is from the vibrational frequency of the God Force, the slower the creative process. This gives humanity an opportunity to change its creations before the consequences are felt.*

[4] *Had an Earthean enjoyed playing in the waters of Earth, he might have manifested fins and scales. Someone who enjoyed the freedom of the air might have created wings and feathers, much as people today put on scuba gear or use equipment for hang gliding. No big deal; one just had to envision or hold the thought of what was wanted. Unfortunately, as the frequency was lowered, Eartheans often became entrapped, lacking the patience to undo what they had done. If your mother ever warned you against making faces "or your face might freeze like that," then this may be a buried cellular memory of this long-ago time.*

Chapter Two

More Changes

God felt the pain of the Eartheans, but, due to the choice of separation, could no longer send the vibrations of love, harmony, encouragement and hope throughout the very essence of their existence. Humanity had chosen to change the vibrational channels. It had exercised its right to choose and was now living with the consequences. Eartheans had shut off the vibrational frequency of unconditional love. God spoke words of comfort, but humanity heard not. They knew of God's love but could feel it not. Eartheans suffered much during this period, for they knew it was all their doing. They judged themselves and assigned blame, for they knew it was their *fault*. They willing punished themselves for their actions.

They knew of what could be. They knew of the abundance. They knew of the pleasures that had once been, but they were caught in a web of their own making. The more they struggled and resisted, the deeper they sank. They began to feel helpless. Guilt, shame, blame, and doubt were meshed in humanity's existence. These, too, were, and are, Earthean choices. These, too, only served to lower humanity to the depths of despair.

Eartheans knew (for they were not yet veiled) that this was all part of God's Divine plan, so they began to feel that it was God's plan to have them suffer. Sorrow surrounded them. The shadows of darkness enveloped them. The light that had once illuminated Earth was now dimmed, as Eartheans wallowed in self-pity.

Still, free will was God's gift to Eartheans. Free will was Divine law on planet Earth. And this was good, as the Divine plan always is.

The God Force felt the pain, the sorrow, and the grief. It was endless. God pondered long on the plight of humanity. It was decided that intervention was needed. Those that helped create this wondrous plan were called forth by the God Source to alter the original creation.

Changes were made on behalf of humanity. God's infinite wisdom and mercy altered the Earthean existence. The integrity of the Divine plan of free will went undisturbed. Eartheans would still be responsible for their choices and the consequences of those choices, yet the changes would assist in giving humanity new choices and new opportunities to begin a new. And this was good, as the Divine plan always is.

Change One: Stabilizing the Earthean Form

As the Earthean frequencies lowered, the ability to move in and out of the physical forms was lost. They had become entrapped in their own imperfect creations. They could no longer experience the joy and freedom of moving in and out of physical form. Those on Earth who had not become encumbered by their choices saw the misery of those that had and were concerned that they, too, might become stuck by the same process. They recognized that if they moved in to *fix* or to *judge* their Earthean companions, they risked the consequences of this interference. Therefore, many of those who maintained their vibrational frequency integrity simply moved to other planets to enjoy growth and to avoid the vibrational entrapment which was occurring. They knew that those they left behind were learning the lessons of choice, as mandated by the Divine plan. They trusted the Divine plan and the wisdom of

God; they allowed and honored the individual path of all humanity and judged it not. And this was good, as the Divine plan always is.

God could feel the shame and embarrassment felt in the hearts of those who had not maintained their frequency. But interference, even by God, was not allowed, according to the Divine plan. Humanity had to experience the consequences of their creations upon the once wondrous and beautiful Terra, or they had to ask for assistance. Only then could help be given.

Beloved Mother Earth had been created for the Eartheans' pleasure. Humanity had co-created with God, but the original perfection had been defiled with now-hideous creations (as was being judged by those who created these forms) of their own making. Their own once-perfect form was now defiled*. For this they were truly ashamed.[1]

God wanted to ease the pain of these beloved children, so God altered the existence on Earth but did not and would not interfere with free will. First, God intervened on their behalf because they had so requested. The alterations that had changed humanity's original form were removed. The God Force once again provided a standard body form that still allowed for the diversity needed for free will. Then, with loving kindness, God simply erased the alterations. (There were some Eartheans who chose to keep their unusual physical alterations and, thus, those have existed through much of Earth's history. Stories of these creatures, such as the half-man, half-horse, still exist in mythol-

[1] *Humanity still carries much of this shame for physical form because of deep remembrances of this period. This is not needed, for indeed, the God Force had purified it once again. Yet shame is a choice; therefore, Eartheans are free to choose shame, under the laws of free will.*

ogy. Only when it was the Earthean's individual choice was their form altered.) Because of the lower frequency that Eartheans now carried, it was no longer possible to move in and out of physical form; therefore, the body became a permanent reality.

This is the point when Eartheans began to identify their own existence with their body, to see themselves *as* their body. They lost the ability to separate from their body—mentally, emotionally, and physically.

With the new, standardized, physical form, these beings could now, within God's new guidelines, begin again in whatever manner they chose. This is also the point where the "God, help me" prayers began on Earth. Eartheans had lost the ability to alter things with just a thought, so now they began to plead with God to do the things they no felt they no longer could. They had forgotten they were designed to be the co-creators with God. But still it was their choice. And this was good, as the Divine plan always is.

Change Two: Separation From Higher Self

Other adjustments were made to the nature of life of Earth. The God Essence gave humanity a new choice. This new choice allowed Eartheans to leave a greater part of their soul essence on the other side of physical existence. This greater part of self would remain in the higher-dimensional frequencies; thus, it became known as the higher self. This higher self would be able to maintain a higher perspective of the Earthean existence. The higher self would always be in Divine frequency. This higher self could adjust awareness in order to maintain constant contact through intuitive channels, no matter what the vibrational level of the physical being. This higher self could be the cheerleader, the teacher, and the guide, but the physical self[2] always had the last word. The physical self had the choice to heed and follow the guidance or not.

It was also arranged for this higher self to be able to have direct contact on a regular basis; therefore, *sleep* was introduced to humanity. The physical body was thereby given a period of inactivity during which the higher self was given time and opportunity to teach, preach, or counsel in whatever manner would best serve the individual. Dreams, nightmares, direct instruction, and other methods of guidance came into existence. This separated part of the self would allow each being to guide self in everyday decisions, yet it would not interfere with the laws of free will. It was still self guiding self. And this was good, as the Divine plan always is.

So it is today. As one becomes more in tune with the higher self, which is always attuned to the God Source frequency, less sleep is required. Sleep time is often used, instead, as a time to alter frequencies, make adjustments in the physical structure, or to provide advanced teachings.

Change Three: Opportunities for New Beginnings

The next change brought the time/space continuum to Mother Earth. The God Source felt that there needed to be cycles of beginnings and endings. Opportunities to start anew were needed by the Eartheans who continued to beat up themselves for their bad choices, as they perceived it. Therefore, time was introduced. It provided for the

[2] *The "physical self" often refers to the totality of life on Earth. The physical self is a combination of the physical (emotions), the mental (intellect), and spirit (God self). The mental or intellectual body has also been referred to as the ego or personality. Humanity is now in transition from moving beyond the limits of the physical body or the mental personality into the unlimited greatness of the God self working in harmony with the totality.*

illusion of a beginning, middle, and end to exist on Earth. The birth-death-and-rebirth cycle was created, as well as the night-and-day cycle. Seasons of the year and lunar and solar cycles were used to create this distortion of the real reality. This allowed Eartheans to begin anew with each day and with each life.

The birth-death cycle would include an opportunity to be re-educated to the steps needed to raise oneself from the lower vibrations. This would provide an opportunity for humanity to learn how it had "missed the mark"[3] (as they perceived it) and alter the future choices. God would not diminish the consequences of the choices that had been made thus far, but with these new changes, it was hoped humanity would make fewer self-destructive choices. Teaching humanity about the steps needed to lift its vibration between experiences would, perhaps, alter the outcome without altering the process. Better prepared, Eartheans would rejoin those on Earth to try again. And this was good, as the Divine plan always is.

Change Four: Humanity Was Veiled From the Greater Awareness

It had been very painful for humanity when full awareness was given. Therefore, another change was made—a veil was placed over the conscious mind of those on Earth. With each new beginning, they truly began anew, because the memory of the past was wiped away. God wished to spare humanity from any further despair. Only by going inward, to the essence of who one truly was/is, could full knowing occur. Only by going inward would the greater truth be shown. Only those who sought the greater truth would be given it. Only those who

[3] *"Missed the mark" is the original definition of the word sin.*

could find the inner strength and were prepared to handle the greater truth would be given it.

Humanity would be taught valuable lessons on the nature of life on Earth between lives, then returned to the Earthean schoolhouse, in order to try, try again. Over and over, God provided the love, guidance, and light needed for this physical journey. The patience and love of the God Essence are infinite. The God Source judges not, for all is but an experience or opportunity to experience. Life is but a Divine game, and all is but an opportunity for growth. The Divine plan had determined the rules that were followed on Earth. And this was good, as the Divine plan always is.

Change Five: A Separation of Sexual Identity

The Divine Intelligence brought into existence man and woman. Earthean physical form had previously existed, but without gender. In the beginning there had been no separation in the Earthean form, for none was needed. All were one with the God Essence and equal. All had full opportunity to be or do whatever they pleased, as long as they were willing to reap the consequences of their decisions. But the God Essence wanted to provide an opportunity for Eartheans to raise their vibrational rate. This would provide them an opportunity to choose to come back into universal vibrational attunement. Therefore, humanity was given a new choice. Eartheans could now choose to come to Earth in either male or female form. Females were destined to be the great receptors; they would be given very sacred rites of procreation, in harmony with Mother Earth. Whereas the male forms would be the great providers; they were to provide the seed of initiation. The forms were equal, only different. Each would provide new opportunities for creation and growth. Sexual intercourse was created as a gift to humanity—a way to express unconditional love to self and others. The sexual climax was to be an opportunity—a flicker of re-membrance of the total God Essence in vibrational memory. At each remembrance, the vibration would be raised. This, indeed, was a great gift. And this was good, as the Divine plan always is.

Free will was in effect, however, and Eartheans did not feel de-serving of this wondrous gift. The limited, physical, conscious mind could neither accept nor understand it. This wondrous process of sex-ual union was, therefore, reduced to what could be handled, manipu-lated, and understood by them. Love is all-encompassing, but a finite mind can not comprehend it.

Sex became the earthly manifestation of *love*. They understood not the meaning of unconditional love, so they created a conditional, physical experience which they could comprehend. That, by Eartheans, could be understood.

Over time, the sexual experience would also be used to con-trol, dominate, and manipulate others, but it was not the original in-tent. It was meant to be an unconditional sharing of God's love. In the sharing, they were truly allowed to experience the frequency of the oneness.

But free will allowed the Eartheans to choose how the sexual union was used. Control, dominance, and manipulation appealed to humanity's inward need to punish and be punished.[4] The choice, again, was in the hands of humanity. And this was good, as the Divine plan always is.

Eartheans were given many opportunities to raise their vibra-tional frequencies so that once again they could be reconnected to the universal consciousness; but, alas, they chose this not. Instead, they chose to feel self-pity and misery.

[4] As the sexual union became associated with the lesser qualities of humanity, then those "of God" felt that all sexual union was bad. It is not. It is simply one small expression of an infinite expression of Divine love. Sexual union is neither good nor bad. It is only an experience that reflects what is in the heart. If what is in the heart is not of the highest, most pure, then the sexual act is like coarse sandpaper on fine silver. It mars the sense of self-greatness, self-love, and worthiness. The damage can be great. But the act, when combined with a pure heart and with no thoughts of dominance, power, control, or aggression, is a wondrous process of combining energies so that both people are expanded, and it takes those involved into a greater connection to the God Essence. The vibrations of both are raised in such a manner that neither will ever be as they were, but much enhanced with their brief exposure to the Divine, unconditional love vibration. Therefore, a partner for a sexual union should always be selected with great care and after great thought. If this is not done, then the reverse is also true.

As humanity used the sexual union in a destructive manner, it was decided that having a single partner would allow humanity to experience the benefits without the destructive encumbrances; thus, monogamy was introduced on the planet. As humanity moves back into the vibration of unconditional love, then the sexual act will again be enjoyed for the single purpose of sharing the Divine frequency with another. No concern for permanent attachment will be necessary, for all will be one.

Procreation of life will occur by choice of intent and not as a result of the physical act.

This brought about a greater lowering of vibrations and more extreme consequences. Just as Eartheans had once known that they were a part of the great universal God Consciousness, they now knew they were not. For eons, however, a sufficient number of Eartheans had chosen to remain in the light and in vibrational harmony, and, thus, the collective, Earthean frequency remained high and balance was maintained. As those who chose lower vibrations began to grow in number and those beings of the light chose to leave the Earthean influence, this state of balance was altered.

This collective consciousness or mass consciousness is the collective frequency of all who are a part of the Earthean experience. As this collective consciousness was lowered, it, in turn, affected all. This lowered frequency caused all creation to take on many of the attributes of the *lesser light*, which came to be the label associated with those who lowered their frequency. The beasts became more aggressive. Eartheans began to experience fear for their safety. Death began to be perceived as an awful, permanent experience, whereas before, it was merely an experience, an opportunity for a new beginning—a vacation of sorts.

Pollution was brought to Terra. Eartheans could now see the outward manifestations of their inner reality. They had defiled their vibrational heritage and now this was manifested in their world. No longer were the consequences of their choices simply manifested in their individual lives, but now the collective consequences were projected for all to see. It had been hoped that through this magnification, the need for new choices could be easily seen. But these manifestations and the threat of even greater consequences of collective Earthean vibrations went unheeded. The lesson went unlearned.

Humanity began to refuse to accept responsibility for their choices. They blamed their life circumstances on everything outside themselves and refused to make new choices that would alter these circumstances. They denied that they had the power to create their own reality. Yet this was free will in action. Eartheans had been given choice and this was, indeed, their right to choose. Eartheans' choice was the denial of their right of choice. This was truly free will in action. And this was good, as the Divine plan always is.

Humanity continued to punish itself. Eartheans continually brought into their existence all the lesser experiences, as if to prove they were unworthy. This was not needed. This did not please the God Force, but it was the right of humanity to so choose. Therefore, it was allowed. It was, however, in violation of God's original intent for Earth to be a great place of joy, love, and harmony. Physical existence was meant to be a playground of opportunities, but, instead, it had become a heavy experience of self-punishment. Humanity had forgotten joy and had taken life seriously. This was not part of the original plan, but it was humanity's right to choose.

For the first time, God did not feel it was good; suffering was not intended. Still, it was the Divine plan; therefore, it was allowed.

The God Force knew the eventual outcome of these combined Earthean choices, yet would not violate this perfect plan. All choices must be made as a result of free will by each individual in residence on Earth. Yet Terra was being defiled and would eventually be destroyed if humanity continued along this path. Terra, too, was a living creation. Terra, too, had chosen to co-create with the God Source this playground of physical existence. But neither Terra nor God had foreseen the choices the Eartheans would make, and now the vibrational consequences of these choices were having a terrible effect on Terra. Something had to be done or Terra would not/could not survive.

Once again the God Force intervened. A call was sent throughout the universe and beyond. Mother Earth, beloved Terra, was in trouble, and volunteers were needed.

Many heard that call. Those who were followers of the Living Light and resonated to the universal Divine frequency heard that call. Those who emanated the Divine love radiance responded with speed.

A great conclave was convened. And this was good, as the Divine plan always is.

Chapter Three

The Great Conclave

Many heard the call from the God Force. The call was clear. Beloved Terra was in trouble, and without assistance, total destruction would eventually result. There were those who tried to ignore the call, but when the God Force speaks, it is unmistakable. Throughout the universe and beyond, many went inward to listen to God's message. Many searched their hearts for the true reason they wished to serve. All knew that if they helped for the wrong reasons, it would help not. A great conclave was to be held on behalf of the planet Earth. All knew of the importance of this gathering. Legions began to gather for the conclave. So it was that many were called.

The conclave was held in what could best be described as an indoor, sports-type arena, with massive seating all around the perimeter and special seating in the center. Every seat was taken—no, every inch was taken—for the arena had standing room only. The excitement, love, and enthusiasm that filled the air were breathtaking. The electricity caused by this collective, highest vibrational frequency charged each in that assembly. *Everyone* present wanted to be a part of this mighty plan. *Everyone* present wanted to serve the God Force and Terra.

The volunteers included dignitaries from all corners of existence. The Council of Twelve, the Masters, and the Light Sisterhood and Brotherhood were all there to show their support and learn how they, too, could assist with the Divine plan. Angels and archangels filled the arena. The neophytes, or those relatively new to the service of the God Essence, were honored just to be in the presence of this grand assembly.[1] Beings from all dimensions attended, including many who had been involved in the development of Terra and her Divine plan. Those in attendance were willing to give up all in order to serve the Living Light.

The call for assistance was for Terra, not humanity. Eartheans, after all, had made the choices that had brought themselves to this sorrowful state. They also had access to the knowledge needed to bring themselves out of it. All that they needed was to forgive themselves, eliminate their judgments of self and others, trust and allow the Divine love that radiates forth when allowed, ask for help, and then go within and listen to the guidance given. Humanity had only to relax into the

[1] *The assembly was not in what would be recognized as human form only. Those who gathered had forms of every variety. There were beings who were pure light. Some were waves of color that changed to reflect inner thoughts and outer happenings. There were beings who seemed more animal-like, and there were tall, short, and in between. The movie, "Star Wars," had a cantina scene with a variety of intergalactic species that were somewhat like the varieties represented in this conclave. All radiated the higher vibrational frequency of love and universal harmony. All came as humble servants of the God Force. There were no "hot shots" or egos present. All knew and trusted the Divine will. All knew that what was decided there would serve Terra in the highest degree. All were brothers and sisters of the God Force. Therefore, the differences in their outward appearance went unnoticed, while the Oneness of all was unmistakable.*

will of God, trust, and "let go and let God." (This works as well today as it did then.) No, it was not humanity that needed assistance, for it had free will. It was the beloved planet's collective, vibrational frequency that was being altered by those in residence, and Earth was helpless. Earth needed assistance, but to best assist Earth, humanity would need to raise its awareness of the universal God Force.

No, the call for assistance was for Terra, not humanity. Those in the assembly knew it was the Mother Earth they were to assist. Earth, after all, was unique in all the universe, and the Eartheans were resisting, thus bringing on themselves great pain. The volunteers knew the Oneness of all the universe; therefore they, too, felt the pain. They could feel the pain of beloved Terra, because Terra, too, had a consciousness. All wished to assist in releasing this anguish and, once again, raise the vibrational frequency.

The list of magnificent speakers included those of importance throughout all the universe and universes beyond universes. Many spoke of the events that had brought Terra and the Eartheans to this critical place. Others spoke of the current Earthean conditions. Still others spoke of what was needed. But all of this detail failed to dampen the spirits or the desire to help among those in attendance. In truth, it only served to make them more committed than ever to this very special project. Finally, one of the great Lights, Lord Sananda, rose to tell of the sacrifice that would be made by those who agreed to the Earthean assignment.

Lord Sananda Speaks

Dearly beloved, we are gathered here to talk of great sacrifice. We are here to talk of what actions are needed to prevent beloved Terra from being totally destroyed. You see, those of Earth do not realize where they are headed, nor understand the total destruction that is being brought into their reality by their collective choices. Earth has not been prepared to handle the low vibrational frequencies which humanity is bringing upon itself. Eartheans are busy licking their self-inflicted wounds. They are busy scratching out an existence. They are busy with the concerns of the flesh. They have forgotten the joy of reunion with the God Essence. They have forgotten how easy Earthean life was meant to be. They have forgotten all that God has provided to bring them joy and love. They have become tangled in the web of physical illusion. They have brought to themselves pain, and they realize not that this pain is but illusion, that it exists only in their minds. They have forgotten the wondrous reality that exists, if they would but see.

The God Force has provided much and intervenes often in order to awaken those who yet refuse to see and hear of these gifts of abundance; but alas, this, too, has failed. Many decisions have been made on behalf of humanity that will be important to Terra, yet will not interfere with Eartheans' free will.

You, my dear brothers and sisters, have come to be a part of this. God has willed that the suffering and pain experienced on Earth shall not go on for eternity. Therefore, a date has been set. Either Eartheans will awaken and recognize their foolishness, or those who do not shall be removed and allowed to continue their foolishness on another planet that has been prepared for this and is better equipped to deal with the lower vibrations. Those Eartheans who do awaken will move into the Living Light and love of the God Force and realign themselves to the universal consciousness. These shall herald the wondrous time of bliss on Terra. As it was in the beginning, so shall it be forevermore.

Many trumpeters will be sent forth to assist in the awakening of humanity. This is the role you will play, my loyal comrades, but it will not be easy. You, too, must be transformed into Earthean form, for the fate of Terra can only be determined by those in residence. In your heart this may sound easy and without challenge, but I shall warn you, it is not. The entrapments on Earth are many. Those of you who agree to serve will be protected and assisted by those on the other side, but you also must be willing to hear with your inner being or your service will be useless. As time goes on, I shall prepare you for this service. We shall discuss now what is needed, for there is much to do and much more to discuss.

If you are chosen to serve, you will be making a long commitment to your Earthean assignment. You must prepare many times and rehearse your roles until the appointed hour arrives. You must feel all the pain and suffering humanity has ever felt, in order to help ease that pain. You must find your own way through the darkness until you find the light. You shall tell others how you are doing and what you are doing in order to best serve them. You must serve still others who have come to serve Terra. You shall have many masters during this process, and you must be a willing servant to all while maintaining the integrity of your own elevated vibrational frequency.

This is not an impossible job, but it will be most challenging. On many days you will ponder why you have volunteered at all. You will long for the comforts and the freedom of home, wherever home may be. Even then, your conscious memory of home will not exist. The home you seek will not be found in a place but in the state of vibrational attunement to the God Essence. You will seek comfort in humanity, but none shall be found. You will turn to your God Source in despair and there, dear friends, will you find all you seek.

You will want to share and teach others with words. This will not work, for you must teach with your life and from your heart. Your joy will be contagious. Do not force another or try to convince them your truth is best or the one and only truth. You must avoid the entrapments of judgment. Know that if you infringe upon another's free will, you have created the biggest trans-

gression of all, for you have violated the heart of the Divine plan. This you must not do!

No, you will model for humanity with your life. You will raise your Earthean vibration to that of love, peace, and harmony. Then, like a tuning device, you shall raise those Earthean vibrations around you. You shall speak of your God Essence with such personal experiences that those in your presence will seek to also know their God Source. You must and shall slash through the self-forged chains that bind Eartheans to the lower vibrations. Then you shall teach others who ask how they, too, can break through. This ripple of light and love, small at first, will grow until all of Earth breaks out of the misery that Eartheans have chosen. Then and only then will Mother Earth be healed by those in residence, for their vibrational frequency shall heal her with little trauma.

This will happen, but it has not been determined whether it can happen before the appointed hour arrives. If it does, then you will have served Mother Earth and the God Force well, for the new day shall be gently and lovingly ushered in, as on the wings of the butterfly.

If it does not, then you shall be on Earth to assist those others in preparing for the new day, which will arrive with great trauma and chaos, as understood and gauged by Eartheans. And those who do not allow the Living Light will be transported to their new beginning so that they, too, will continue to search for and find their way. Mother Earth will then go through a cleansing to wash away the residue of those of the lesser light. She shall again be revitalized with the frequency of universal love and harmony, of the Creator's abundance and perfection. This is the nature of the new day on Earth! Terra deserves this and so it shall be. So be it!

A thunderous applause filled the air. Lord Sananda had told the story of what was needed and what the volunteers' role would be. His heart was filled with love, but there was also concern for the fate of Mother Earth. For he, too, knew that the task was, indeed, formidable, and that he, too, would make sacrifices in order to serve Mother Earth. *Giving up your personal Oneness with All-That-Is is the supreme sacrifice. That, indeed, was what was being asked from each volunteer.* And the reality existed that if these volunteers became entrapped in the heavy Earthean vibration; if they, too, failed to see the illusion of their Earthean physical life; if they, too, failed to take time to go within to gain counsel from their higher selves and the God Force; then they, too, could become part of the problem instead of the solution. They, too, would remain forever entrapped in the life-death-life cycle of humanity. They, like those on Earth, would remain entrapped until such time as they, too, would again be awakened to All-That-Is. The dangers were many and these volunteers knew it.

There were many speakers, and much inspiration and information were given. Finally the appointed hour arrived. The announcement of those selected for special assignment was to be made.

Those who were being chosen now would take on the most weighted role[2], bear the heaviest burden, and assume the greatest responsibility. They would have the most powerful impact and have the most opportunity to serve Terra.

This, the volunteers knew, also carried the greatest danger, for they would be the most obvious targets for humanity's hurts. They would have to take on the most pain and suffering in order to show the lack of power that pain and suffering has over who they really are— children of the Living God Force. These chosen ones could either cause humanity's greatest growth or get caught up in the illusion and cause the greatest harm. Still, those in attendance trusted and were eager to serve the God Force. If they were needed, they would serve and they were ready.

The conclave was silent. A stillness pervaded the very essence of every being in attendance as each one went inward to listen to the God Essence. Even then the God Essence spoke with a wee, small voice, but these beings were the best at hearing and heeding this inner guidance. They knew, and knew that they knew, and they trusted this knowing.

As all turned their thoughts to God and listened for God's whispers, the very conclave began to resonate at the vibrational frequency of the universal God Essence, with an intensity that few in attendance had ever before experienced. All in attendance were truly at-

[2] *All who serve God are important and have important tasks. There are many roles and many universes. No hierarchy, as understood and judged on Earth, exists. Those who have the most experience are given the most responsibility, for they have proven themselves worthy.*

one-ment with All-That-Is. The ebb and flow of all creation was felt in that gathering. The entire conclave began to resonate with the love and knowingness of the God Force.

There were no speakers at the podium. The stillness in the conclave was beyond everyone's experience and imagination.

No sound existed, yet each volunteer heard and heeded the wee, small voice from within. The calling of the God Force was loud and clear, yet silent to the ear. Thus, the God Essence began to call those in attendance into service to Mother Earth. The call was unmistakable, yet spoken only from the wee, small, inner voice.

Solemnly, with awe and reverence, those who recognized this inner call stepped forward. They would later be known as the *core volunteers*. With great honor, they mounted the podium to share what they knew of their role during the next eons of time on Earth, for in their call to service was encoded much information. There was great emotion, for they were humbled to be chosen. Both the volunteers and those in the audience shed tears, openly and with joy. Each recognized the glory and the obligation which this choosing symbolized. Each knew and trusted the wisdom of the God Force; therefore each trusted that they would be worthy of their Divine mission.

Words cannot accurately convey what transpired in this conclave as the chosen were called forth. A brief but powerful period of silence followed the selection of each of the chosen ones. Following this silence was the selection of those who would work with and support that core volunteer while on Earth assignment.

With a vast, synchronous movement, those who would serve the chosen ones rose and moved silently to the side of their dear comrade. These would serve as their earthly council while on the physical plane. They would be the ground troops who would serve by their side throughout the eons of time on Earth. The Divine Forces would always be on the other side of physical existence, but the troops would be with them in physicality. They, too, would share in the accolades, respect, and honor of service to the Divine Force, and they, too, would share in the responsibility.

This core volunteer and his/her ground troops made up each volunteer unit. Each unit knew it had been given a specific responsibility. Each unit knew of the importance of its role and mission on Earth. They fully recognized that to be successful in their missions, the volunteers would need both Divine and physical support while on Earth. They knew that while in the Oneness of creation, but they also knew they would be veiled as they entered into the physical body and would have to rediscover this vital information while in Earthean form. They would be given all they needed, but there was no guarantee they would hear the Divine council, for it spoke in a soft, inner voice. They would also need physical support, and it was hoped that they would provide this for each other.

The volunteer troops knew, too, that it would be the core volunteers who would draw the most fire and have the most extreme experiences while in the physical. They would be the ones to suffer the most from the difficulties of physical existence, in order to break through the illusion for the greater good of humanity. The core volunteer would have little chance of success without the backup troops. All of the volunteers would serve the Living Light and would thus become known as the light workers of Mother Earth.

Those chosen first were, indeed, the core volunteers, but each had a small troop of committed and specialized volunteers to assist, and all would be important to the vibrational reclamation of Terra.

The selection and identification of the chosen was repeated many times, as one by one those who were to carry the responsibility of Mother Earth's survival stepped forward. Yes, it was a crown of glory placed on their head that day, but on many days to come, it would feel as if it were a crown of thorns.

As each volunteer was selected, there was an outpouring of love and a deep feeling of consecration felt throughout the conclave. Those who received their assignment simply moved forward to share. Those who were assigned to assist each volunteer also moved forward. Each had an opportunity to address the assembly and share their feelings. Then the groups, these unbelievably powerful units, left the gathering.

Silence filled the air as each assembled unit departed. They departed to pray and listen. They departed to prepare for this great Earth mission at hand.[3] They departed to search their souls, for they would need to know themselves well to do God's bidding.

There was no comparison or coordination of plans between groups, for they knew that the plans would be given in accordance with Divine will and they would follow regardless of what they contained. The volunteers had long since learned to exist in the moment, trusting that they would always hear the murmur of Divine spirit and

---

[3] *These tasks could easily be accomplished in the pure form, but they must be completed while in the physical. Herein lies the difficulty. That is the reason why many lessons are needed and help is given on a regular basis. It is the physical mind and body that must be altered in order to resonate in Divine harmony with the soul essence. The spirit essence needs no preparation, but the physical processes must work together. The body, mind, and soul must meld with the God Essence/ Spirit Force. This melding must occur while in the physical, before the Earth-based volunteers can truly be the right hand of God.*

have the courage to follow it. They trusted, although they did not fully comprehend the challenges of living in the illusion of the physical. All trusted that the God Force would provide everything that was needed. They trusted, and they accepted, and they loved greatly.

This slow progression lasted most of the day. All knew this was important and was not to be rushed. All knew that the silence and stillness of the day underscored the great sanctity of the experience.

Indeed, many were called to this great conclave, but relatively few were chosen for the great Earthean mission. Humanity's remembrances of this conclave would stand through time. Many were called— few were chosen. The chosen ones would now begin their volunteer service to planet Earth. Thus, their home base would now be Terra. The Earth-based volunteers had been identified and they had willingly stepped forward to do their part for beloved Terra. With great intensity, the Earth-based volunteers now prayed for guidance, strength, and wisdom to conquer the Earthean entrapments. They and their Earthean mission would last through the eons of time—until the beloved Earth was healed and she had regained her original status and vibration.

After a period of prayer, there was great fellowship. After the fellowship, the conclave was reconvened. Many addressed this prestigious gathering to express their joy, their love, their appreciation, and their expectations for a bright future on Terra. Lord Sananda again addressed the gathering:

> *My beloved brothers and sisters, it is with great pleasure and honor that I join with you on this day to recognize what the future may hold for all of us. We have been told of the many obstacles that lie in our path. We have been warned of the distractions. We have been shown that this will, indeed, not be a fast or easy mis-*

sion. But we, as children of God, know that there is no other way. We move forward to free the hearts and souls of humanity from the shackles of illusion. We, too, must experience these shackles firsthand, running the risk of becoming lost in the process. We, too, must repeat the Earth cycle over and over, until we are sure that we can awaken at the appointed hour to free all of humanity. We shall have many rehearsals throughout history. We shall experience much along the way that shall prepare us for our final hour. But we shall have a great partner at our side. The God Essence shall ever be in our hearts to assist, and when God is on our side, we must reign victorious. Blessings to all. Go in the comfort of knowing all is in Divine order.

This time there was no thunderous applause. There was silence and deep contemplation, and slowly the arena emptied. There were many embraces, tears, and a silence that united each person present. All those attending this great conclave would remember this experience, for it would be forever-etched in their very souls. The memory could be suppressed, but never erased.

The Earth-based volunteers had come forward to take their place on Terra.

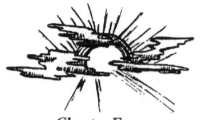

Chapter Four

Enter the Earth-Based Volunteers

These great Earth-based volunteers were ready; after all, they had prepared in every way possible. They had listened to those of Earth, they had listened to the counsel of wiser, more experienced Elders, but mostly they prayed and listened to the teachings that came from within. These were the true, personal teachings of the God Essence. They knew that what they would miss most was the loving, caring, and always joyous vibrations of love that came from the God Force. The God Force had been with them from the beginning. After all, what would existence be like without the conscious knowledge of It? Yet they knew they would be without It. They knew that they would again feel the love, but they must first journey through Earthean existence to find the way home, back to their true home where their beloved God was waiting.

     The volunteers did not fear failure, for failure was impossible. In fact, they did not fear, because fear is impossible when true, unconditional love is present. But they did wonder what it would be like to venture so far from home—home, where the universal consciousness resides; home, where the awareness of the Oneness of all resides; home, where the true connection and Oneness with the God Force resides; home, the vibrational frequency of love and the Living Light; home, the state of being ever in a state of total joy and bliss.

The volunteers did not all jump into physical existence at once. Like the adolescent that reluctantly leaves home, so, too, did many volunteers venture away from their home.

Slowly, the first and most confident volunteer ventured into physical form and the lower frequencies. Birth was not the immediate entrance used. No, that would come later. They began this experience slowly. They would first try maybe just a brief trial visit—a few years in a willing Earthean's physical form; a young one, at that: a child, where silliness can be explained; where few expectations exist. After all, how hard could it be?

The volunteers pondered long and hard on the strangeness of physicality. Their thoughts were echoed by many who would later enter into physicality, but the first must always light the way for others to follow.

The first volunteers who entered into the Earthean form pondered the strange sensations of physicality:

How strange the sensations! The body is so confining. It moves, but with great effort. It has a variety of sensations—some pleasant; some not so pleasant.

How do I control the mind? It seems to be independent. It puts thoughts into the body as it desires. What happened to the total serenity? What happened to simple existence? These are such strange thoughts. They distort the silence. I long for the silence, where Oneness occurs.

An animal is heading for me. I'm running; the physical body is taking charge to avoid pain. Doesn't it know that pain does not exist? Of course not; that's why I'm here. But there are so many complications. So many things to do RIGHT.

I thought that as a child it would be O.K., but it's not. I have hard work to do, but the body wearies; yet, that's right, that's right. I remember now—the body requires sleep so I can go to get counsel. Thank God, such a welcome relief! I can rejoin my wondrous Creator, my source of comfort. But the respite is over so quickly.

And everything is so confused. I fear for food. Will there be enough? The pain...the body can bear it... but...my soul, my very essence, longs for home. Why does it have to be this way? Why can't I just assist from the other side? Life is so hard! The physical demands so much attention. It feels pain and it thinks it feels joy, but it's not true joy. Poor thing...it knows not what is missed.

And the mind, it fights so hard for control. Why, why, dear God, does it not know that only by surrender to your loving Divine Grace can it truly reach its full potential? Only by giving up can it achieve access to all. Why does it not remember that as long as the mind and body control and choose the path, it remains forever locked in these lower vibrations? Only by letting go and giving in to God's will, can humanity be lifted. God wants only the best for humanity. Why does hu-

manity not see? Why does it not remember? Why do the mind and the body war so for control? Why do they struggle for dominance when all can be achieved only through harmony with All-That-Is?

The soul is there; so is the spirit. And buried beneath it all is the loving God Seed, the power to be all. It seems so easy, yet it is not. Dear God, help me; take me out. I need further preparation. Why is this so complicated? Why are there so many distractions? Why can Earth-eans not see? Thank God I can again feel the love, the harmony, the joy. Oh, how I have missed it! There is no place like home.

So ended the initial entry of an Earth-based volunteer.

After this volunteer's first entry into physical density, many volunteers gathered to discuss, tell, see, hear of the experience. All were interested. All desired to help Earth. But they knew they could not help unless they, too, could cope with the strangeness of Earthean existence. Each wished to help and learn from the others.

The volunteers pondered why Eartheans had put themselves in such a position, and why they kept themselves there. Still, they knew it was not their job to judge, for they knew the final outcome of all judgment. Humanity had been given choices; they had chosen, and they would continue to choose. The volunteers respected the Divine plan, which allowed for these choices. No, the volunteers knew that their job now was to help raise the vibrational frequency of Earth in order to ensure survival of the planet.

After viewing this initial Earthean experience over and over, much as one would study a football film, other volunteers began to venture forth into the Earthean world. There were a variety of reactions. Some loved the physical sensations, such as sex, food, drink, and found them to be full of pleasure. Others became caught up in the race for advancement—could they do more, better, faster, bigger than another? And so it went. Some entered Earth much like children, jumping into a creek to enjoy the splash. Others hated the experience and grew angry and defiant. They demanded to know, "Why should these things happen to *me*?"

All the while, the God Force recognized that each volunteer was experiencing and growing in his/her own awareness of physical density. God loved them all and poured forth love to these volunteers. No matter what the final outcome, the God Source, and all those who labored on behalf of the God Source, recognized and honored the courage and commitment these volunteers had shown in agreeing to be a part of this Earthean rescue mission.

After each initial physical life experience, they all gathered together to learn and prepare for the next experience, much like those who parachute gather on the ground to offer their congratulations and to share in the excitement of a first-timer. The first time someone jumps out of an airplane and lands safely, it is remembered and celebrated, just as the volunteers remembered and celebrated their first entry into physical density.

The volunteers were beginning to see how humanity had become entrapped. When they were *home* (as in their Divine frequency), they knew physicality was a game, and a silly one at that, but it was so easy to get trapped by the power of the illusion which made it seem real. They studied hard. Each descent into matter caused the volunteers to become more determined to help. Each became more resolved to bring light and love to Earth. Each became more determined to help in whatever way possible.

Often, in these early descents into Earthean existence, the Earth-based volunteers had chosen rather uneventful lives—no one important; no one of great consequence. Although each, in his or her own right, was a superstar in their native land and in the eyes of God, here on Earth, each had to struggle just to exist. Still, this was their finest hour. This was the beginning of their struggle on behalf of Mother Earth. And then they rested until they again chose to reenter the heaviness of Earth.

Other, more courageous volunteers, chose lives of power in which to introduce great learning, great wisdom, and light into the Earthean frequency. They made many contributions *IF* they avoided judgments, for if they moved into judgments, they helped not.

Others choose the slower path to influence, by experiencing lifetime after lifetime, until at last the volunteers could enter Earth, live, love, then exit. Nothing tough; just simple. As they mastered this with speed and efficiency, (gradually at first and then with greater speed), they chose more important roles. With each life, they selected more responsibility and chose to deal with more entrapments—a little power, a little prestige, love, children and families, wealth—and so it went. Each began testing self with one element of Earthean distraction after another until they were sure of themselves, and they were sure they could still operate with unconditional love. They knew that it was not the Earthean distractions themselves that were the problem, but their *reaction* to them. The Earth-based volunteers had to avoid becoming entrapped by these distractions. Wealth did not have to be associated with greed and the fear of losing it. It could also come with generosity, love, joy, and abundance. If a volunteer abused power in one lifetime, he/she merely backed up and tried again during the next life, knowing the lesson would become more complex.

Finally, after many Earth experiences, these Earth-based volunteers felt their readiness to tackle more. Now they felt themselves to be ready to begin to influence humanity and the Earthean vibration. Many treaded slowly at first, but steadily. By example, they showed Eartheans compassion, how to grow, how to assist Mother Earth and each other. As they were able to renew their connection with God, they moved forward faster in their lives, becoming the great writers, the great scientists, the great inventors, the great statesmen. In each lifetime they raised the vibration a little, and then a little more. They also chose lifetimes as orphans and robbers and drunks, for the experience and/or influence. They knew that their lives had to be role models and they were needed in every arena.

Often, the volunteers would cause Eartheans to reawaken to the God Essence and the grandeur of the inner worlds. Then the Earthean, too, would volunteer to serve on Earth, so that, over time, the number of Earth-based volunteers would increase. On occasion, a chosen one would withdraw from service, wishing to serve God in other capacities. This, too, was allowed, for all on Earth had free will.

Earth assignment was and is difficult and always full of challenges. The volunteers who requested release were lovingly granted it and reassigned to other worlds and other tasks. There was no dishonor in requesting another assignment. There have always been many ways to serve the God Essence. On Earth, all had free will, even the Earth-based volunteers. This was the Divine plan on Earth and it was and is perfect. Thus, the status and numbers of volunteers serving Mother Earth is ever in flux.

Occasionally, the Earth-based volunteers did make mistakes. They got caught up in the Earthean entrapments and forgot to go within and listen to their council. The volunteers even chose lives where they abused power, people, and even Mother Earth. They wanted to know how it felt to stray from their Divine path. They needed to experience the unpleasant sensations attached to these choices, for they knew the time would come when they could not afford the luxury of a mistake, and having these memories in their totality would assist them.

When the volunteers strayed from their Divine intent, they suffered much. The deviation from Divine purpose caused great pain to themselves, for they wanted so much to help—and yet help they did not. They wanted to serve the God Force and assist Mother Earth, but, instead, they hindered. If these great volunteers forgave themselves and moved on, then no lasting harm was done, but if they continued to punish themselves for their mistakes, then they continued to slow the Earthean progress.

Even so, as the volunteers left life on Earth, the God Essence, and all those who had helped in the creation of Mother Earth, were there upon their return to spirit form, to encourage, to love, and to honor these brave legions of light workers. Each lifetime was celebrated, upon its completion.

The volunteers' presence on Earth was beginning to be felt. Often the volunteers themselves failed to recognize their own vibrational impact. They knew what could be if only the Eartheans would surrender to the Divine Force, so they did not always appreciate their own slow but steady influence within the totality of the Earth vibration.

Eventually all the Earth-based volunteers could move in and out of Earthean life, joining the birth-death-rebirth cycle, until it, too, became natural for them. They did not realize this was part of a great cycle when they were in their Earthly existence, for they, too, were veiled from the Divine truth. They, too, would have to struggle with the challenges of life on Earth until they each conquered the maze of physical illusion and once again awakened to the greater reality.

The volunteers often chose to enter Earth life in clusters so they could support each other during these trials and tribulations. Other times they would reconnect with their fellow volunteers later in their Earthly existence. Always, the presence of other volunteers gave them comfort, and they knew not why.

Always they were given counsel, but not always did they listen. Always they learned and grew, but not always did they appreciate this growth. *Always, they turned to God during their darkest hour, but not always did they realize that, had they turned to God first, their darkest hour would not have come.* Yet all was in Divine order and progress was being made.

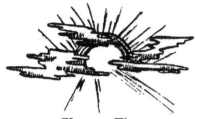

Chapter Five

Remembering Love

he volunteers knew that love was the answer to the woes of humanity. Love was the key that would unlock the chains that held Eartheans down. The Earth-based volunteers tried desperately to remember love as they entered into each new Earthean existence. The Earthean vibrations were so different, so foreign to the universal love vibration—and life held so many challenges, so many distractions—that it was easy to forget the love vibrations, as they entered and reentered the Earthean world.

The Earth-based volunteers tried everything. They made arrangements with fellow volunteers before they entered the physical. They hoped that meeting on Earth with another volunteer would trigger a remembrance, and sometimes it did. They arranged to have special events come into their lives. Sometimes disasters would cause them to turn to God. Sometimes it was great abundance that would help them to remember the abundance God had intended. All these events worked sometimes, but at other times nothing worked. There were no easy answers or quick solutions. No matter how they schemed, connived, or plotted prior to entering the physical, it remained an individual choice to be made while on Earth and in the physical. Being in the physical form seemed to change everything.

Choosing love was easy *outside* physical density, but much more challenging while *in* the physical. In order to choose love, one had to move through all the distractions and illusions. One had to remain focused on the reality of the God Source and the *real* reality, before one could move into the universal vibration of peace and harmony. Earthean existence did not often support such basic beliefs. Instead, Earth encouraged competition, materialism, and greed. Control and manipulation were lessons more easily taught on Earth by those in residence. Indeed, it was a challenge for the volunteers.

The Earth-based volunteers knew that if they could remember unconditional love, it would trigger a greater remembrance. Thus began a process of becoming obsessed with love. Love on Earth was different from love outside the physical. On Earth, it was a sexual or emotional experience, such as male/female love, love for an object, or love as a reaction to some pleasant event. But true, unconditional love was different. It simply *was*. Earth love was a reaction *to* something. Unconditional love is. It is not limited to a person, object, or event. Unconditional love radiates from the God Force within. It is honoring and respecting all as part of the One. All energies that come into contact with this unconditional love vibration are affected by it. Unconditional love transforms all to a higher vibration. The Earth-based volunteers knew this when outside the laws of the physical. They tried to remember it while they were in the physical.

Unconditional love on Earth was difficult to achieve. Earth-based volunteers would sometimes become obsessed with one form of love or another. Many became the great lovers of all time, settling, in Earthean form, for a brief exposure to the God Force vibration while in the physical.

Love in the physical became a playground of opportunities to explore. The volunteers enjoyed the experience, as did their partners; but there was always an emptiness when it was over, for the true essence of who they were recognized that these games were really searches for something deeper, something more meaningful, something they did not yet understand while in the physical. *They were still in search of the way home, for it had to be rediscovered during each lifetime and within the given set of circumstances that lifetime brought.* The way was difficult, but they knew in their heart of hearts that love was the light for that journey. Thus, the search for love was always a part of each Earthean experience.

Eartheans and the volunteers searched for love, but understood it not. They used the word "love," but understood it not. Eartheans had not learned to experience and/or express unconditional love; therefore, few models existed. Even so, the volunteers were gallant in their attempts to bring unconditional love into the vibration of humanity.

While in the physical, they understood not that love is, indeed, something that starts in the universal God Presence. Between physical existences, they could understand that love is the glue that keeps all matter together.

They understood that when humanity failed to feel love, they felt scattered, not together. Humanity does feel love, but what *is* felt and what *could be* felt is like a blade of grass compared to a giant California redwood. Humanity has failed to allow love to expand, grow, and flourish, so that it could be the great force it was designed to be. For if humanity could only operate in love, no rules, no police, no armies would be needed, for no one could do anything to hurt or harm another. No hate, no fear, no guilt, no judgments, no self-doubt could exist, because these would not be in harmony with universal, unconditional love. These lesser qualities simply could not exist, and Earth would, indeed, be a beautiful world to "love" in. Under the law of free will, however, it must come from each individual's choice, not imposed from someone or somewhere else.

Light workers—the Earthean volunteers—had chosen to come to Earth to help. They knew all about unconditional love, until they entered the physical. On Earth it was easy to forget. It was easy to encrust God's love essence with concerns of ego, of self, and of the physical.

> *What if I'm taken advantage of?*
> *What if they think I'm silly?*
> *What if no one loves me back?*
> *What will people think?*
> *What if...What if?*

These were some of the ego concerns that plagued humanity. The volunteers, like the Eartheans, had to choose love while in the physical.[1] If only they could remember that choice is not really necessary, that all they have to do is surrender to their natural state! *This natural state of unconditional love flows freely if it is but allowed.*

Between Earthean lives, the volunteers were given instruction. During meetings with their council and during periods of sleep, they were shown the way; but upon arising, the conscious mind ruled, and it did not always wish to allow the unconditional love to pour forth, for it feared losing its position of importance. It feared for all the "what ifs."

Some volunteers did, indeed, find love. Those who did found a state of bliss that few could relate to. They moved into the state of being in the vibrational frequency of unconditional love. This was the vibrational frequency of *home*, of the God Source, and in that state, they found everything.

[1] *Light workers have chosen to come to Earth to help. It was more difficult and time-consuming for the first light workers to allow the unconditional love to flow forth, but much faster for those who followed, for they had the great teachers and the love essence to ignite them. The first volunteer for each lifetime stumbled to find the path. Then they illuminated the way for others. That's why the volunteers had been carefully selected and guarded and given very important life lessons.*

Some struggle more than others, but they need to feel the resistance, for they are sent to work with those who resist the most. If they did not know how real the struggle is that rages inside, they would not be as effective with their followers. The lives of the Earth-based volunteers have often been filled with doubt and with trials and tribulations, for they need to feel the struggle and remember it well. The time shall come when they will be the most trusting and the most sure. They might become impatient with others who are slow in their awakening to the truth of All-That-Is, had they not experienced these same resistances. They must sit and bring forth the memories of their struggle and be able to laugh. These volunteers clear the way and illuminate the path so that others may follow. These awakening volunteers are in all walks of life; they may be teacher, garbage collector, housekeeper, or tollbooth attendant. They can be easily recognized, for they radiate a special love, and one feels uplifted just being in their presence. Anyone who allows unconditional love to flow through his/her life and essence is a volunteer in service to the planet Earth.

When humans existed in this vibratory place, they created a force field around them that is truly Earth- and life-changing. Much like a tuning fork which, when struck, causes all things in its presence to also resonate to the same frequency, these volunteers assisted all in their presence to resonate in turn to the God Source. The Eartheans who came into the presence of the volunteers who were carrying the Divine frequency did not fully understand what was happening to them. They knew that when they were with the volunteer, they felt better and life was more complete and joyous. The unawakened volunteers were drawn to this frequency like few others, for they craved what it had to offer them...home.

Thus, the enlightened volunteers were sought out for their company, for they carried the frequency of the Living Light. The volunteers who had allowed unconditional love were always surrounded by others. Depending on their Earthean mission and station in life, they might have had followers, supporters, subjects, or simply friends. But always, the unconditional love caused the volunteers to move into a life shared with many.

A shared life is a life of service, and the volunteers fully understood this. Although others may have felt they were serving the volunteers, it was the volunteers who were serving the Eartheans.

The Earth-based volunteers had come into Earthean existence to serve Mother Earth and the God Source, for they knew that their greatest source of joy and growth comes through service. They had found all they sought through unselfish service.

They served all by radiating the Divine frequency. This frequency radiated out from their very essence. It became part of the planetary mass consciousness—the totality of all frequency on Earth. When this happened, it raised the collective consciousness on Earth. This was healing needed for both humanity and Mother Earth.

These Earth-based volunteers often served the Earth by giving up their privacy and moving into a public life in which there were many demands placed on their energy. They moved into public awareness in many ways, as great teachers, writers, actors, politicians, and as leaders in every field of endeavor. As the public felt their great vibration, they were sought out. Everyone wanted a piece of what these special volunteers had, and that was not always easy for the volunteers, but it was always willingly allowed. Being in the public eye allowed the volunteers to model for all. The volunteers knew that by giving of themselves, they allowed others to move also into their greatness. By giving of themselves, they knew that others would find their way through the Earthean world of third-dimensional illusion. This was a great and wondrous gift...they truly gave of themselves.

As the volunteers opened to a world in which they had greater influence, they knew that the influence came from the God Source, which they willingly carried on behalf of Mother Earth. They knew it was not them, but what they shared on behalf of God, which was the object of the admiration. The sought not for followers, but lovingly touched all on behalf of the God Essence. Thus, the greater good was served.

These volunteers drew much criticism and attack from those who rejected the Divine frequency. Nonetheless, the volunteers knew that it was often important to be the grain of sand in the oyster shell of the Eartheans' existence, and *that* was their *important job*. They knew that being the source of aggravation could be the catalyst for growth, change, and beauty. So they did not attempt to be what everyone wanted them to be, but, rather, tried to stand in their Divine God connection and *be all that they could be*. They did not try to *not* ruffle feathers, but sought always to stand in their own truth in all ways, including vibrationally.

The volunteers feared not for their own well-being during these times of drawing criticism and attack, for they trusted the power of light and love. They knew they carried the frequency of the God Source, and in this, came the assurance that all was in Divine order. They had surrendered personal will to that of Divine will; therefore, they knew that only that which would serve the greater good could occur in their life. They feared not for their physical well-being, because they knew that if they were physically impaired by acts of violence, this, too, would serve the greater good. Over the Earthean history, many of the volunteers willingly experienced martyrdom. Some are still being read about in history books, thus still serving the Divine cause. They knew that with this Divine vibration, random violence could not occur in their presence. Nothing is stronger than the vibrational frequency of light and love, if it is held in integrity; therefore they knew that those who wished them harm were powerless in their presence. Yes, these lesser lights could inflict damage, but it would have no effect on the totality of their existence, unless it served the God Source. These Earth-based volunteers knew that regardless of what occurred to their physical body, they were beyond the reach of humanity's touch. Thus, they feared not the issues of mortal humans, for they knew they had the protection of all creation.

This fact alone caused great concern among many Eartheans, for there were those who wished to control and manipulate humanity. But because the volunteers were without fear, they were impossible to control through threats of violence and death. The enlightened volunteers were without judgment; therefore they were beyond the use of shame, doubt, and/or public disclosure as control techniques. Because the enlightened volunteers used no techniques to control or manipulate others, they were beyond the influences of all methods of control. They simply existed in their power of Oneness. Try as others might, nothing could induce these volunteers to behave in any way inconsistent with their belief structure.

Many enlightened volunteers were sent to their death because they feared nothing, including death. Volunteers were often seen as threats by those who wished to keep Eartheans in servitude. Those who wished to end the influence of the volunteers rarely saw the significance of their action. Rather than end the influence of the volunteer, death usually inspired greater influence. When volunteers gave up their lives in the line of duty and for the greater good, they were given more responsibility and power in their next Earthean experience. Those who sought to put out the flame of truth only empowered it.

Earth-based volunteers learned of the true power of love and light as they moved into the Oneness of the Divine frequency. In times of trouble, they had been told to "send love" or they had been told to "love their enemy," but these words took on new meaning as they radiated this frequency. *They knew that to send love was to send out a vibrational energy field. The energy field affected all in its presence.* To send love to a place of disharmony was to give all in that location a vibrational choice. This energy field often caused peace to descend on the area even though few understood why. The volunteers willingly sent this powerful force field to places of hate, fear, and unhappiness, as this broke up the current energy field and provided the residents in that place an opportunity to make new choices. This acted much like cosmic Drano. It caused the energy to begin flowing again. But those in its presence were free to make the same choices that clogged it the first place. Therefore, by sending love, the Divine plan of free will was never violated.

The volunteers knew the power of this field. If sent to plants, they grew faster and fuller. If sent to people, it caused a sense of well being and peace. If sent to food, it changed the molecular structure so that it became more nutritious and stayed fresher longer. If sent to wild animals, they became tame.

The volunteers knew, too, of the dangers of using this force field. If used in a wrong manner or with wrong intent, the same power that was used for good could backfire and destroy those who used it. This was done when the love vibration was used for control and manipulation. *Unconditional love meant that the love vibration was given without strings or motive. It was freely shared with all, including one's enemies, to be used in any manner desired by the recipient.*

If love was sent to fix something, then it was conditional love and no longer served the greater good. Love sent to a perceived enemy, for the purpose of making him/her a friend, is conditional love, since it comes with strings. In essence what is being said is, "I will give you this love if you use it only in the manner I outline."

An employer who sends love to a troubled employee to help him/ her become more productive or relieve the employer's burden is sending conditional love. An employer who simply sends love to a troubled employee is sending unconditional love. No outcome is being embraced, thus there are no strings to the gift of love; no conditions are presented with the gift.

A friend who sends love to heal a sick friend is sending conditional love. This may be well-intentioned love, but it is conditional nonetheless. A friend who simply sends love to a sick friend is sending unconditional love. Love, light, and God all carry the same frequency. Therefore, sending God's blessings carries the same power as holding someone in the light or sending unconditional love.

Conditional love comes with strings, expectations, and motives. Thus, the recipient must use the energy field only for healing, or relieving burdens, or whatever purpose was intended. *This is a form of manipulation and/or control, which is a violation of free will.*

The Earth-based volunteers use this incredibly high love/light energy to serve the greater good; therefore, they offer their love and light to all who need, desire, and want it. They offer their own vibrational frequency of love to all who are in their presence, not to fix or alter, but to provide the opportunity for all to willingly choose the light and love of the God Source, which is the place of great joy, peace, and harmony.

As the Earth-based volunteers moved into this vibration of love, they moved into a reunion with the Divine Source. This reunion allowed them to have access to the collective, universal consciousness of all that has occurred on this planet and beyond. Much like a giant computer filled with all the knowledge in the world, this consciousness contains all wisdom. Like a computer, which must be entered, then requested to give forth information, so, too, one must seek the answer from within and it is given. The seeking of answers in the place of one's center acts to unlock the information, and, while the vibrational alignment gives one access, possession alone does not cause the computer to release its treasures. The enlightened volunteers knew this and understood the access process for all wisdom. They knew they knew what God wanted them to know. They trusted in the wisdom of the Divine plan of which they were now a part.

In this place of center, the volunteers learned to seek counsel with All-That-Is on all issues of importance. They learned to access the great minds of all times and from all universes. In this vibration of Oneness, they learned that they had earned the right to take their sacred place among the magnificent ones of all creation. They had earned their place of honor, for love had caused them to break through the Earthean illusion and connect with their own greatness and source of power. Once the vibration of unconditional love and light had been attained, all was laid open before the volunteers, for now they had the wisdom to use and understand the totality of creation.

This was, indeed, the reason the volunteers had entered the Earthean experience. In this powerful vibratory state, the volunteers began the awesome task of anchoring heaven on Earth. They knew that heaven was not a place, but a vibratory state of being. *Heaven was being in Divine connection with the God Source.* Heaven was, indeed, the dwelling place of the God Source. When the volunteers moved into the state of love, they existed in heaven while living on Earth, and they illuminated the way for others to enter this magical kingdom while in physical embodiment.

The Earth-based volunteers were given many procedures and techniques to assist them in raising their individual and collective vibrations and being at peace with their earthly existences. Because water was so abundant on Earth, it was often used to trigger this remembrance of peace and love. Water, or the image of water, would serve as a reminder to go with the flow, to blend with All-That-Is, to move with the ebb and flow of Earthean experiences.

The following images and directions were given to, and were often followed by, the Earth-based volunteers, to their greatest advantage. You may choose to bring forth the images and memories as you read.

> *Sit and bring forth an image of beautiful, lush, green grass, calm and peaceful. Your breathing is slow and deep. Each breath draws in the God Essence. In that essence is found the unconditional love vibrations. With each out breath, you release all that no longer serves you. Ask the angelic helpers to assist you in breathing in that which serves you and releasing all*

that is restricting and or limiting. This vibration is the energy of the universe, the Oneness of All-That-Is. Breathe it in. As you exhale, you breathe out the tension and the heaviness of the Earthean vibration. You feel the peace and harmony of All-That-Is. Feel the love of Mother Earth. Continue the breathing and allow your thoughts to turn to love as you allow your consciousness to begin to float over the green fields before you.

As you look out over the grassy knoll, you see a beautiful, clear, natural spring of crystal-blue water bubbling from the ground. It bubbles forth, bringing you a sweet sensation of joy and peace. The water is the vibration of unconditional love. As you watch, the spring seems to respond to your joy. It sends forth more water, seeming to come alive, in response to your appreciation. The beautiful, crystal spring of love pours forth more water. Now it is a small fountain rising a foot or more out of the ground. You continue to watch and find pleasure in the watching, the joy of your experience pouring forth from your heart. This again empowers the water, that knows only the joy of its existence.

Again, the spring adds more pressure to its flow, and it rises several feet from the ground. The spring is now a small fountain rising from Mother Earth. The more love, joy, and appreciation you feel, the more the fountain is enhanced. Over and over this cycle is repeated, until this fountain becomes a massive geyser that rises hun-

dreds of feet from the ground, washing and purifying everything it touches. As the beautiful, pure water cascades over your body, you feel a warm, loving, tingling sensation throughout every cell. It is a wonderful sensation, and you can feel the negativity and lower vibrations being washed away. With each drop, you feel the difference, as each cell of your body is filled with loving vibrations. Each cell explodes with love; your heart sings with joy.

You send your appreciation to the fountain. The fountain is again empowered, and it again grows until its flow of purifying water washes the whole of the world. The world, too, feels the gentle cleansing of its lower vibrations, and all of Earth tingles and responds. You stay in the vibration of love and light for as long as you choose.

This waterfall is symbolic of the God Essence sending forth love to humanity. All humanity needs to do is simply receive and appreciate the gift. As Eartheans continue to appreciate this wondrous flow of universal love, they begin to feel a small bubbling in their very essence. *The essence of humanity is the God Force love vibration,* but it has been encrusted with layer upon layer of choices at an Earthean level. Eartheans who recognize God's gift of love create a small crack that allows this love to pour forth. Humanity's reaction to this small spring of love will determine whether it grows or closes up, leaving it sealed once more in the layers of illusion.

If Eartheans will but watch and allow this spring of love, it will grow until it becomes the mighty force that washes away the lower vibrations from all it touches. Eventually this force could heal the entire planet.

Eartheans' reaction to this small bubbling-forth of love can be varied. Some see it as weakness and quickly patch the crack; others fear that this joyous feeling must be of the devil, for they believe God desires a serious and stern world. Some quickly look around for an object for this wondrous love, feeling that whoever their eyes gaze upon must be the cause. If humanity would but allow this spring of love and empower it with thoughts of appreciation, what a world of joy would emerge! But, alas, in the physical there are so many distractions—so many reasons to seal the cracks, or so humanity believes. These distractions turn minds away from contemplation and the realization of the perfection that is humanity's heritage. If only the volunteers and Eartheans would sit and allow the memories to flow forth! These memories would force their opening to the light and love of God, enabling Eartheans to truly *let go and let God.* All are taught to go within, but relatively few heed the advice.

The Earth-based volunteers know all of this in their heart of hearts. Their higher selves, who remain in constant contact with the God Essence, know this. When not in the physical, they know that what is created by God is real, and what is made by humanity is only an illusion that can be quickly changed. But while in the physical, these volunteers get caught up by the illusion, believing it to be real. Thus, the cracks that allow love to flow are often patched over to better protect themselves from the Earthean pain. If they would but let the love flow, there would be no pain.

Lessons of love were often the most challenging for the Earth-based volunteers, but always they contained the biggest reward when mastered. The focus of much of the Earth-based volunteer's life was on allowing love. Many were able to choose love...some did not. All were allowed to choose, as this was Divine plan. And this was good, as the Divine plan always is.

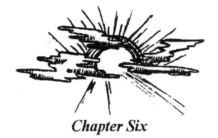

Chapter Six

Releasing Fear

*T*here were (and are) those on Earth who resist change. Even though life was not always pleasant or easy, it was always comfortable. Most Eartheans knew what to expect on a day-to-day basis. Change often seemed uncomfortable; therefore, it was avoided and even suppressed.

There were (and are) those on Earth who feel they have the system beat. They have accumulated great material wealth. They have mastered the art of manipulation and control of others. They care not what the long-term consequences are, for they live for immediate pleasure. They use the process of reward and punishment to their own advantage. They honor not the unique life expression in others, but always wish to bolster their own position. These people resist change, for they wish not to lose their status in life.

Those who seek control and avoid change often work actively to block the volunteers who have moved into the vibration of love. Those who resisted love knew that fear was the way to keep things unchanged. The security of sameness was their desire.

Unconditional love is the highest frequency that humanity can carry while in the Earth plane. Fear is the lowest frequency that can be experienced and still maintain life. Fear also moves very erratically, whereas unconditional love moves very smoothly and evenly. Many have said that the opposite of love is hate, whereas others have maintained that the opposite of love is indifference. Neither is correct. *The opposite of love is fear*. The phrase "scared to death" is a real possibility. Fear reduces the flow of energy. Enough fear can cause the physical body to die.

Those on the earth plane who wish to keep others controllable have done all within their power to induce fear in them. They attempt to trigger fear and portray a menacing world. They show Eartheans that they must always guard against evil, for evil is always lurking to attack. Justifications for fear are given in the news, movies, stories, and television. Those who wish to keep fear as a primary motivation for action know that when people are in fear, they are easy to manipulate and control.

When the volunteers are in the frequency of unconditional love, they are in their place of power. They are connected to the God Source, who supplies them with all information and inspiration, through the wee, small voice of intuitive guidance. They are in the universal flow of wisdom. Those in the flow do not concern themselves with what is right or wrong in a societal sense, because they judge not right and wrong. They follow their Divine guidance in all situations. This is why those who are truly connected to the God Source have been feared throughout history. Those in the vibration of unconditional love are uncontrollable, from an Earthean level, as they take instructions from the highest Source.

When the volunteers are in the frequency of fear, they are in a place of weakness. They are totally disconnected from their source of all information and wisdom. They get no inner guidance because they cannot hold the frequency necessary to make the connection. Therefore, all behavior decisions are based on the object they fear. If pain, either emotional or physical, is what they fear, then decisions are based on avoidance of pain. If poverty be what they fear, then all decisions are based on avoidance of poverty. Those who fully understand the nature of Eartheans know that by understanding what humanity fears and then carefully choosing fear-triggering words and actions, the Eartheans are totally at their mercy and control.

While in fear, Eartheans have no emotional strength. While in fear, Eartheans possess no wisdom. While in fear, Eartheans have no compassion. While in fear, Eartheans have no Divine protection. While in fear, however, Eartheans can have incredible physical strength, as the nature of the fight-or-flight adrenaline system provides it for short duration. Thus, armies are conditioned with fear so they can go out and kill the enemy with brute force. Fear is the reason for so many random acts of violence on the Earth, for it turns rational people into self-protecting animals who feel they must destroy the other person before they, in turn, are destroyed.

Fear can also be induced by special implants. They have long been used on Mother Earth by those who have self as a prime motivation. These small devices can be mechanical, crystal, or etheric (without physical form). All serve the same purpose—to scramble the vibrational frequency of the person and to make Divine connection much more difficult to attain. Without the Divine connection, maintaining a love frequency is impossible. Without the love/light frequency, Eartheans are pretty harmless and controllable. The implant may be operational all the time or only sometimes.

The implant that is only activated at times is the easiest to detect. Its sporadic functioning often makes individuals wearing it appear to be extremely moody. They act and feel one way when the implant is not functioning and quite another way when it is active. They may experience peace and mental clarity when the implant is off and confusion and anger when it is on. Through their own power, they are helpless to alter the frequency shifts. Earthean medications are ineffective against the effects. Individuals who are plagued by these implants, however, often turn to illegal drugs to mute their effects. Eartheans who are troubled with sporadically active implants know there is something wrong with them because they have a point of comparison. They can feel the difference between implant activation and deactivation, although they may not know the cause of their problem.

The Eartheans who have implants that are always activated are not so lucky. They have come to believe that this muddled mental state, this state of confusion, is natural for them. The always-on implants are not as strong as the off/on implants, but they are just as troublesome. Instead of experiencing wide mood swings, these people experience a life of muted frequency. They never feel good or joyful or peaceful or harmonious or loving. They are forced to experience life through a very uncomfortable perception. These Eartheans often turn against God, because they feel God is punishing them and they feel unworthy of His love.

Those beings responsible for the implants, both from Earth and other worlds, look for moments of weakness and take advantage of each moment. Nothing can be done without the Earthean's permission because that is the nature of free will. But permission can be given in unusual ways. Words have power, and, spoken loosely, can have great consequences. When Eartheans utter the phrase, *"Something is bothering me,"* either in statement or question form, they have given permission for something to bother them. Their words have opened the door of possibility.

Earth-based volunteers were (and are) prime targets for implants, for those who understand, know that these volunteers have great power and heavenly support, and that if they move into their power, Earthean existence will certainly be altered.

Many volunteers have learned how to recognize and neutralize the impact of an implant. Although several removal techniques exist, the easiest is to lie quietly and ask the angels to remove the implant (and anything else that may be affecting their vibration) from their be-ingness. The angels remove it from the etheric body, and when removed from the etheric, it cannot exist in the physical. The volunteers feel the shift in vibration almost immediately. They often feel the same weakness and dizziness that accompany Earthean surgery. Always there is a shift in frequency and mood. The volunteers also know to ask the angels to protect them from further vibrational influence *which is not for their highest and best good.*

If any volunteer or Earthean wishes to be clear of any outside influence that is not for their highest and best good and the highest and best good for all concerned, all they must do is become receptive, by sitting or lying quietly, and ask for heavenly assistance. All things are given to those who ask and believe. After this angelic surgery, give the angels permission to do anything and everything needed to heal the area and prevent any further influence for these lesser-light sources. It takes only a few minutes and the effects can be felt.

Earthean nature is that of a creator. It is their heritage, for they are born of a Creator God. The Bible reads, "In the beginning, God created...." The free-will nature of planet Earth empowers the creative side of the Eartheans. Unfortunately, they do not retain the full range of choice afforded by free will, because they focus on what they fear, thus bringing the object of their fear into their life. By fearing something, they manifest it into their reality. *Free will does not mean that only what an Earthean needs or wants is given.* Universal laws do not judge. *Eartheans are given whatever they will.* Will is put out into the creative flow of the universe through thought. *Whatever an Earthean thinks about is manifested.* Since fear causes the Earthean to think about what is feared, that, too, is manifested.

Thus, fear is a block to unconditional love. Fear cuts off the flow and restricts the process. Fear also creates that which is not desired. Eartheans and the Earth-based volunteers have had to learn to release, not suppress, fear. Only then can universal love exist in the physical.

To resist fear is to empower it. Therefore, the Earth-based volunteers had to learn to release and move beyond the effects of fear. They were challenged to learn to accelerate their energy even in the face of fear. They learned to take action and hold loving and compassionate thoughts and feelings even when facing fear. By taking action and responsibility, they neutralized fear's power.

Fear was used to keep the volunteers subdued in their power. Thus, one of the most important lessons the volunteers had to learn was how to release and move beyond fear in order to stand in their power. Once in their place of power, they were the mighty force for change that they had descended into the Earthean vibration to become. In their place of power, they could anchor the heavenly vibrations to Mother Earth. In their place of power, they could heal and transform Mother Earth to her own place of power.

Chapter Seven

The Reality of Illusion

𝕿he apparent reality of illusion soon proved to be one of the Eartheans' and the Earth-based volunteers' biggest problems. When not in the physical, one could easily distinguish between what was real and what was illusion, but this was not so on Earth. The body's senses were great deceivers. Illusions could be felt, heard, seen, tasted, smelled, and perceived with senses not yet understood by humanity. When the senses told the mind that things were real, then they became real to them. Yet real they were not.

The Eartheans had been given the power to co-create. God created. Humanity could create by using the powers of the God Force to co-create. What was of the God Force was real, for these maintained the essence of the God Force. These things had permanence. What was created by humanity did not. When Eartheans lived in harmony with All-That-Is, it was easy to discern what was of the God Essence and what was not, but as humanity began its descent to the lower vibrations, it became much more difficult to discern reality from illusion.

If the Eartheans had gone within and asked for the gift of discernment, it would have gladly been given. They did not. The illusion was so real that they didn't realize they needed to.

This process of humanity's creation is much like the process children use to create a fantasy world. Children use blocks, boxes, and other odds and ends to create a town, garage, farm, or other place of adventure. They create what they are thinking about. Then they play with these structures for as long as they have need of them. The child is totally absorbed in that play. They behave as if these creations are real. They may even fight to defend these creations if someone calls them unreal or tries to dismantle them.

An adult can easily see these are not real; they are a fantasy first conceived in the mind of the child. The child merely pulled what was needed from the environment to create this pretended reality. This creation has no permanence but does serve a purpose by allowing the child to experience and to grow from that experience, at the child's own level of understanding.

When the child's need for that experience ceases, these self-created illusions are either recycled into a new experience or discarded. Adults don't worry about this type of children's play because it contributes to a healthier life—it is through play that children learn to make sense of their world. Play is one of the most powerful processes for growth, and children know this intuitively.

But if these same children became so wrapped up in this imaginary play that they lost sight of it as play and became totally absorbed, 24 hours a day, and felt it was real, then a parent would become very concerned for the child's welfare and would do whatever necessary to break the fantasy that engulfed the child.

And so it is with humanity. On a grander scale, humanity has been given the power to bring its thoughts into existence. Eartheans create their world in order to learn and grow at their own level of understanding. It is a wonderful opportunity. Unfortunately, humanity has become convinced that these creations are real and that things beyond his/her creations and senses are unreal. Eartheans have become totally engrossed in this play, to the point where it is no longer in their best interest. They have forgotten that their experiences were designed for them to play with and grow from. They no longer find joy in them. Eartheans' creations are causing much pain and disharmony because people attempt to gather as many things as possible. Eartheans act as if they win the game if they gather the most stuff.

The Earth-based volunteers themselves had to learn, and then help Eartheans to learn, that, indeed, *life is a game created in the mind and brought into existence by the gift of free will. This game was meant to provide growth and joy.* It was not meant to be taken seriously and cause humanity to become entangled in the web of illusion.

Had Eartheans understood the energy forces and how they worked in the physical, they would have understood why the illusion seemed so real. These powerful forces had been an integral part of the Divine plan for Earth. These forces gave total free will to humanity, including the ability to perceive thought, activate choices, and manifest them into physical existence.

Manifestation was the key that would allow humanity to experience the consequences of their free will. Humanity has a vibrational energy force that draws together "physical essence"[1] from the air to form matter. *The more attuned they are to the universal love vibration, the faster the creations become physical matter. The lower their vibrational level, the longer it takes to physically manifest. This is a safety device installed to protect humanity from its own power.*

Because the time is near, these governing desires, which slow the manifestation process and protect Eartheans from their own choices, are being neutralized. Thoughts are manifesting faster than ever be-

[1] *No word exists for this substance.*

fore. This speeding up process is necessary for the Earthean transition. Humanity must become aware and responsible for all that is in their existence.

These manifestations, or illusions of reality, were the elements humanity needed for pleasure, punishment, or whatever lesson they desired. The ability to manifest physically[2] was the heart of the Divine plan. This ability allowed humanity to reap the consequences of free will, and as long as humans were in harmony with Divine love, it was a source of great pleasure.

The ability to manifest allowed Eartheans to turn thoughts into physical existence, even misery and disaster. They needed only to observe their surroundings, their friends, their life circumstances, to know on which things their minds lingered.[3] Eartheans have yet to lift their eyes to all the beauty, light, and joy that is their birthright. They have yet to see the real value of living in harmony with All-That-Is, for when they do, joyousness will be their existence.

Humanity and the Earth-based volunteers must learn to separate reality from illusion. Since thought creates illusion, humanity had to learn how to deal with thought and how to distinguish thought from truth.

Reality is truth. Truth is of the God Essence, whereas thought creates illusion. Humanity's creations are but illusion. How had the Earth-based volunteers learned to separate thought from truth?

This was to be a difficult lesson. *Volunteers had to give up thought in order to know truth.* Not all thought, just the random, critical, and unsolicited thought. These types of thought actually changed or altered truth as it entered the consciousness. Truth *is*, while thought is merely a process of manipulation. Thought creates, conforms, evaluates, judges, and applies. Truth is. One is a process; the other is not.

[2] *Currently, this technique of visualization has reawakened in Earthean consciousness, and it is being used to manipulate the physical world. Businesspeople use it as a tool for success. Many use it to eliminate bad habits or to lose weight. These are examples of how Eartheans take the wondrous and use it in such a limited and constricting way. And the poor souls who can't "see" mental pictures with their inner eye feel they are doomed to failure. Do they not know that perfection takes many forms?*

[3] *The exterior should never be judged, for the highest, most evolved Masters have often come back as poor, wretched souls (judged by Earthean standards). They may choose this lifestyle in order to have contact with a new population and to move relatively unnoticed. No, the way to see into and measure your life is to ask how you feel about it or look at the fruits of your labor. Are you happy and content most of the time? Are you able to bring joy to others? Is your life progressing the way you want it to? Do not use money or material gain as the yardstick for Earthean success. It is illusion and can be easily swept away.*

Eartheans spent much time thinking about truth. In reality, as they thought about truth, they changed it to suit their physical existence. Thoughts are a matter of choice; they could be changed. Eartheans had to live with the results of their thoughts—their illusions.

Truth is to be accepted, not analyzed. Eartheans have spent many years learning and refining the thought process. Indeed, much of their own reality and identity has been built around thoughts.

Yes, for humanity, it does seem strange to discuss the thought process as something to *shed* in order to know truth, yet that is what must be done. Through thoughts, Eartheans look at things from all angles. Truth is one-dimensional; it simply is. Eartheans must learn to trust the "is." As long as they think, they are evaluating, synthesizing, and analyzing. This is an indication of a lack of trust in All-That-Is. When Eartheans feel the need to defend truth, they are using thought. When they can accept another's truth and allow another to accept other forms of truth without question, battle, or defense, Eartheans will recognize growth in this area. Truth comes from within and cannot be dictated from outside, regardless of the source. Truth is a gift from Divine spirit, the God connection, and is freely given to all who will listen.

There are many variations of truth. God has allowed for that in the Divine plan. Eventually, all truth will bring you into harmony with the Divine love vibration. This vibration will bring you closer to the light. But the Divine plan is a grand design, not a simple progression from point A to point B. It is a beautiful, complex, intricate pattern that introduces humanity to all energies and all experiences needed for growth. Even though it is not a straight course, it is the best course. When you allow the God Force to work through you, you must allow the greater wisdom to guide your feet. Eartheans represent a great diversity. These different people, with different functions, different growth needs, and different roles to play, have need of different experiences to facilitate individual growth. The enlightened volunteers trusted truth.

Truth is the inner guidance, wisdom, and knowledge of the best course of action while on the individual Divine path. Therefore, the truth for one path may not be the same for another on a different path. Eventually all paths lead to the one true truth... *that all is of God and God is love and light.*

The truth is simple, but the road to it is filled with challenge. The one, true truth is like the hub of a wheel—there are many spokes leading to that hub. The many spokes are representative of the many paths which all lead to the center, the hub, the truth.

It is inconceivable to imagine the many spokes arguing about which is the one, true direction that will lead to the center of the wheel, yet humanity does just that. They honor not the diversity that is the heart of Divine plan, but insist that there can only be one way, one truth, one path, and one voice to lead you there. Even the God Source speaks through many willing servants and functions on Earth through all those who surrender their will and are thus willing to be the right hand of God. The idea that there is only one person and one way is foolish and inconsistent with the plan of God, which has provided for diversity in all things.

When humanity fully understands the reality of multiple truths and multiple paths and thus learns to honor the paths and truths of all others, they will no longer feel the need to correct the path of others. There are those who feel they know the correct action of another better than the person living the life. This is what contributed to the vibrational decline of humanity.

To truly honor the truths and paths of others is to respect and not interfere with their actions, even if the actions may bring about less-than-desirable consequences. Assistance is to be given only when requested by the individual. To force assistance or judge the path and truth of another is to violate the Divine plan.

The vibrational frequency of love and light can always be freely dispensed as long as it carries with it no expectation or intentions. Again it is said, someone who is ill can be sent love and light to use as they see fit. This is in harmony with the Divine plan. Yet to send love and light to a sick person to help them heal is in violation of their path. This action does not honor the right of others to choose sickness as a means of growth. If a sick person has requested a healing, then heal in any way available to that person, including the use of love and light.

Learning to respect the path of others is the first step in learning to respect their truth. Enlightened Earth-based volunteers have struggled with self and mastered the ability to honor the diversity of the Divine plan, which allows for *diversity in all things.*

The Earth-based volunteers had to harmonize the physical mind, which often blocks the acceptance of the truth, for it fears it shall lose its place of importance when truth is fully understood and allowed. The mind must be reassured that it, too, plays a part in the awakening, that truth is not a threat. Without the mind and its thought processes, there could be no free will. The mind must see that the higher self knows what is best. Yet the mind fears for its own survival. It sees itself becoming obsolete, unnecessary, cast aside for the glory of God.

The mind must be assured that it always plays a part in the experience of physicality. The mind must filter All-That-Is into a logical, linear, spatial, and sequential physical experience. The mind is needed in physicality; but it fears that when the totality is again understood, it will be obsolete.

Eartheans can talk to their minds as a loving parent would speak to his/her child. The mind has an existence and a purpose, but it, too, needs reassurance, for it has gotten out of control and wishes to limit what humanity can comprehend. Once humanity realizes what a nuisance an uncontrolled mind can be, it will quickly work to bring it back into harmony with All-That-Is.

The volunteers learned that the misbehaving mind will babble. At a movie there may be a constant dialogue, "They're probably not going to fall off that ledge," "The girl's hair looks funny," etc.

Humanity is not free to simply experience the now because the mind races on like a natty, old busybody or backseat driver. It may remind you of all the things left undone or of all the mistakes or flaws within humanity, or it may try to prove one's superiority over another— that is the mind. When humanity is at-one-ment with All-That-Is, the mind will be stilled and at peace, coming forth only as the situation calls for it. Then humanity will be free to pause and appreciate the beauty of the Earth without being reminded that the garbage has not been taken out. This is when Eartheans will be at peace. They will be able to live in the now and be at-one-ment with All-That-Is. This is part of the mission of the Earthean volunteers—to show humanity how to bring the mind into harmony with All-That-Is.

When Eartheans are at-one-ment with the radiant God Source, then all will work with perfect love and harmony, and the mind will be at peace, no longer in need of the perfect response or the "right" answer. No evaluations, judgments, or processing will be needed, for the truth shall be trusted without question by the mortal mind. Nor will the mind be under the control of illusions; it will be free to create whatever it lingers upon. As the mind comes into balance, the soul will be empowered to work in harmony with all life. Illusions will become transparent, and life will become a reflection of God's gift of abundance.

Truth is only light, love, and the God Essence. Where love exists, there is light. Where the light of God exists, so, too, is there love. Light and love are inseparable and indistinguishable, for they are one. Truth exists outside humanity as well as in its innermost sanctuary. The creations of the God Force exist in the light and love of God; therefore, they are real. Anything that operates outside of this Divine vibration is illusion.

Eartheans, who unknowingly lower their vibrational frequency, choose to operate in illusion. *In truth, humanity is made in the frequency of love and light. Truth is, therefore, humanity's natural state.*

In order to know truth, humanity must trust in the Divine plan and believe in its perfection. It must ask for, then accept, help, for prayers are always answered.[4] Know that all you need will be given. Trust, relax, ask, then go within and you will know the truth. Truth can never be forced upon you from an outside source. Move forward with the love, light, and protection of the most Divine God Force. When truth is known, illusion will hold no power, for reality will be apparent.

[4] *Prayers are always answered if we trust and believe. Sometimes we ask for things that, in truth, are not in our best interests; therefore, we give our higher self permission to cancel them. When we pray for something, let us always ask for "this or something better, for my highest good and the highest good for all concerned." With our limited perspective, we can get ourselves in trouble with our requests, so let us always give permission for our requests to be improved upon. Free will exists even in prayer.*

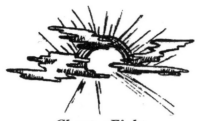

Chapter Eight

Humanity's Game of Life

In the beginning, the loving God Force had seeded the Earth with beautiful beings capable of all things. These beings resonated Divine love. Eartheans had infinite knowledge and capabilities, but they turned away from their wondrous heritage and chose to remember it not.

The caring and concerned God Essence then asked the most Divine from all corners of creation to assist in the remembering. Many of these volunteers, too, turned away from the easy, loving, joyous path in order to stumble along on the jagged rocks of Earthean life.

Somehow those on Earth assumed that this torture, this unpleasantness was needed on Earth to develop strength. The Eartheans believed God had willed life on Earth to be a difficult existence. That was *not* the Divine plan; but it was the Earthean choice. The God Force lovingly accepted humanity's foolishness and continued to send Divine love, in the hope that humanity would someday allow love to prevail.

The God Essence allowed humanity choice, and choose they did. Eartheans chose to compare, to judge, to ridicule, to insult, to jeer and put down their brothers and sisters of Earth. Why? God wondered. Had not the Eartheans been given everything?!

Still the Eartheans chose self-torment instead of God. They chose to compare and judge instead of to love. For the first time, the loving God Force felt frustration about the nature of humanity.

God had given Eartheans the ability to create any life desired. The Divine plan had intended and allowed for physical life to be a fun- and love-filled game. Humanity, however, had written different rules for this game of life.

Somehow, in humanity's distorted illusion of reality, it imagined a giant line that had an hierarchical order. Those of Earth believed that everyone was in this giant line and those in front got privileges. They tried to beat out the person in front of them to move forward. If they could beat out or prove superior to a group of people, then great advancement in position would be gained, or so they believed.

So those on Earth began this new game. They believed this new game had only one winner, and each wanted to be that winner. This game was not in harmony with the Divine plan.

"Beat the Next Guy" was an easy game for Eartheans to play. All one had to do was prove superiority over others. One had to jump higher, run faster, earn more money, have more, think better, control more, be first and win at other such perceived competitions.

Humanity failed to realize that they could, indeed, do this, in terms of the *few*, but not in terms of *all* others. As Eartheans began to look around to judge and compare themselves to others, they saw many things. They looked to their neighbor and thought, "Yes, I have a better job than he," and felt pride. But they also noticed, "Oh, his house is prettier than mine," and felt ashamed.

The laws of the universe are clear: *What you send out must return.* When humans judge others and find them lacking, they must also judge themselves and be found wanting.[1] Thus, Eartheans began to feel the need to catch up. No matter whom they compared themselves to, there were aspects where they were "better" and aspects where they were not. Unfortunately, Eartheans often kept their eyes and consciousness on the areas of "not." Eartheans drifted lower in their vibrations, for now they began to see themselves as unworthy.[2]

For the first time, the loving God Essence wept for humanity. They had been given all, and they accepted nothing. They had been made God's equal, able to co-create in the beautiful world of light and love, yet Eartheans had dimmed their light. Now they even failed to see the Divinity in themselves. They still recited the words "made in God's own image," but they believed it not. Even in this simple statement, humanity had twisted the words to imply that the God Essence had a physical form that resembled its own. Did they not know that the physical, confining form was of their own making? Did they not know that the essence that existed in the inner dwelling of humanity was the

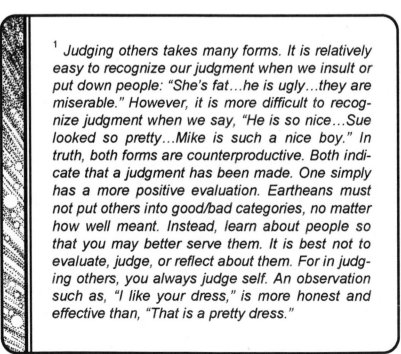

[1] *Judging others takes many forms. It is relatively easy to recognize our judgment when we insult or put down people: "She's fat...he is ugly...they are miserable." However, it is more difficult to recognize judgment when we say, "He is so nice...Sue looked so pretty...Mike is such a nice boy." In truth, both forms are counterproductive. Both indicate that a judgment has been made. One simply has a more positive evaluation. Eartheans must not put others into good/bad categories, no matter how well meant. Instead, learn about people so that you may better serve them. It is best not to evaluate, judge, or reflect about them. For in judging others, you always judge self. An observation such as, "I like your dress," is more honest and effective than, "That is a pretty dress."*

God Essence? Did they not know that was why those who worked on behalf of the God Essence had told them to go within and "know that I am God?" Did not they know?

Of course, they knew not. They had separated themselves from their God Source. They had twisted and denied reality and believed illusion. They could not know this. *And they did not know that they did not know; therefore, they thought they knew.*

Eartheans continued their game of "Beat the Next Guy," for in their foolishness, they were trying to get ahead. They never asked ahead of whom? For what purpose? They cared not, but continued their game. They began to teach their children this game. Children began to compete for grades, for ribbons, for affection, even for attention. The children, too, were taught that when you put down someone, you somehow got ahead. These lessons were seldom obvious, but always present in subtle ways. The children learned the lessons well and then passed them on to their own children.

Eartheans had made many choices. This was their right, according to the Divine plan. But Eartheans had chosen to knowingly hurt another—not just a physical hurt that could easily be healed, but a deep, everlasting, emotional hurt that could last lifetimes. This was inconceivable, but the Divine plan allowed for choice. All of God's creations are linked, and the actions of one creation affect all. Eartheans

> [2] *Self-esteem continues to be one of the most menacing problems facing both children and adults today. Self-esteem is lowered whenever humanity chooses to measure itself using any outside comparison. Only by going within will Eartheans learn of their true greatness. There one will learn of one's own true greatness as well as the greatness of all others.*

had invented a game that lowered the vibration of everyone, for what they sent out would always return manifold.

The more humanity compared and thought themselves superior, the more they judged themselves inferior. The more time they spent looking at the weaknesses of others, the more they became aware of their own.

Eartheans were told many times and in many ways to judge not, yet they did not listen. Over eons of time, many volunteers were sent to shine the loving light on this foolish game, with the hope that it would be stopped. But the fate of this game was always in the hands of humanity. They had created the game, and only they could discontinue it. Interference would not serve the Divine plan; God could have stopped the game, but that would have prevented humanity from discovering for itself the true nature of this destructive Earthean game.

Lifetime after lifetime, powerful volunteers were sent to Earth to illustrate and illuminate another path, another way, another more healthy and constructive game. Often they went unnoticed.

Lord Sananda volunteered to again enter into physical density and shed light on this destructive game. It was hoped that this volunteer would make a difference. The time was right; the people were prepared. This one had the power to make the Eartheans hear, but would they listen?

Many had been sent to prepare the path. They, too, had tried to help humanity see the foolishness of its ways.

This one had resisted the Earthean illusion on many occasions, which was why he was called upon again. He would show humanity what it was capable of becoming.

The God Essence called this beloved Lord Sananda into active status again. This child of the God Essence would become known as the only begotten son of God, but, in truth, he was just one of the many who claimed their Divine lineage. All of creation are born of God, including all of humanity. Not all of God's children are faithful, but Lord Sananda was one of those who willingly served whenever called upon by the God Source.

Terra, beloved Mother Earth, was honored, and she rejoiced in this special presence. She welcomed this volunteer and supported his efforts on her behalf.

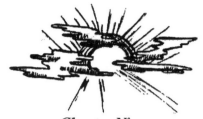

Chapter Nine

Lord Sananda

ord Sananda had had many Earthean walks. In each he had performed admirably, always awakening to the love of the God Force. Always he had performed his Earthean tasks with a directness and swiftness and joy seldom found on Earth. Always he had helped his fellow Eartheans. Always he had lifted the vibrations on Earth. Lord Sananda had been known by many names, and each name had been honored and loved and remembered, as are the names of all awakened Earth-based volunteers.

The God Force now had a special job, and Lord Sananda was the one who could enter physical existence and guarantee its successful completion, for he had broken every chain of the Earthean vibration that held down humanity. Through this man, free will was, indeed, the gift of a loving God Essence.

When Lord Sananda was told of God's plan, he immediately began to prepare. Mother Earth was readied for her special guest. Much had to be done before Earth could receive this great Earth-based volunteer. Heralds went out to tell all who would listen of this great coming. Other volunteers needed for this assignment were gathered and readied. This life would be like no other. Eartheans would *have* to listen, to hear, to see, to feel the love for which Earth was intended. Those workers of the light that had proved to be the strongest, most capable, most resistant to the Earthean temptations were sent to Earth to assist in this mission.

Lord Sananda entered the Earthean form and was given the name Jesus. He would later be remembered as Christ, the Savior, for he came for a single purpose, a simple one. *He came to show humanity the true power of free will.*

Like a stick of dynamite with a very long fuse, Jesus' life would start a process that would cause great change. It was intended that the full impact of his life would be felt in later times, after he had left the planet. The later effects of his presence would light this mighty fuse and cause the breakup of many old patterns of thought. His presence, however, also ran the risk of creating new patterns of mental rigidity that would not serve humanity—but it was a risk that had to be taken.

The plan was clear, simple, and brief, in Earthean terms. Jesus' life was to be a model for all to see and experience (and later hear about). His Earthean vibration would radiate pure light and love so that all who experienced it would be altered. His death would also be a model for those who would learn about it. Since so much misery was attached to death in the physical, Jesus would show the illusion of death. He would demonstrate that death has no meaning; existence is a continuation of one's experience. Perhaps then, it was hoped, humanity would begin to see the Earthean illusion for what it was—simply a manifestation of their own making.

Unfortunately, many continue to believe that Jesus "died for our sins." *Jesus did not die for our sins.* In truth, he lived and died to make humanity free, free of the concept of death and limitation.

Jesus walked the Earth and gave his message of love and brotherhood. He taught those who would continue his teaching after his passing, but, in order to be effective, he had to *live*—indeed, demonstrate with his life—what he had tried to communicate in words.

The words of Jesus were powerful; they shook the very essence of humanity's being. The words even now resonate in every cell of the body. But this was nothing in comparison to the power of the presence of Jesus, the man.

Jesus was able to walk the Earth and maintain the love vibration as few have been able to do. As a result of this vibration, just being in his presence would transform the lives and hearts of Eartheans.

Followers would willingly surrender all Earthly belongings just to be near his powerful aura of love. Those of Earth did not understand this, so they chose to attribute his ability to transform humanity, to his teaching and to his words. Eartheans believed him to possess magical abilities—which, indeed, love has. Jesus wished to show all Eartheans that this special love magic could be theirs.

After Jesus had gained the attention of humanity, then his real task could be completed. He had to die to show death to be but Earthean illusion, and his Earthean ministry demanded that he die publicly. This would convince those who ridiculed him and mocked his message that he was truly dead. His enemies would have no means to claim he had escaped. They could claim no loopholes.

As the drama unfolded, the Roman soldiers, mourners, and spectators played their part well. With so many witnesses present, Eartheans could not deny that death in the physical had occurred. The world would see that Jesus, the man, was, indeed, dead. This was the Divine mission.

Then, just as Jesus had foretold, after his public death, he returned to life. Jesus waited three days to do this. He could have returned to life immediately, but, had he done so, those who wanted him dead would have again "killed" him, for they would have denied that he had died the first time. Therefore, Jesus allowed the illusion of death to prevail. By that time, no one could deny that he had passed on, as the body would have begun to decay. After all, he had been encased in a stone tomb with no food or water, and, under those conditions, denial of death was impossible. Physical death had, indeed, occurred and no one could deny it!

When Jesus "returned" from the dead, those who were his followers should have said, "Yes, just like he said, he's come back. And we can do that, too."

Instead, people fell to their knees and blessed this "only begotten child of God." He wasn't the *only*, but he was one of the few who claimed the powers of God that we all inherit but seldom use.

His return demonstrated that his followers had not really believed that he could and would return. If they had truly believed his words, they would not have been so shocked at his presence after his death.

His followers might have felt, "After all, everyone's prone to a little exaggeration. Sure, he can walk on water, but return from the dead? Hmmmm, that's tough." Even those who accepted the reality of Jesus' return from the dead denied their own ability to do so. They believed not the teachings of Jesus, the Christ, even though they greatly honored the man.

Thousands of years later, Eartheans are still saying, "Wow, Christ came back. Wasn't that special!"

Is it special? Jesus said, "What I do, so you can do also." Does humanity believe this? Never.

Death is still viewed as the Earthean ending. Even though there are countless documented accounts of people who have passed over, returning to share, comfort, or say good-bye, humanity still refuses to believe. These stories are often discounted, attributed to the mortal mind playing tricks.

Many people, after experiencing the death of a loved one, have felt that person's presence. Others have seen and/or heard the loved one. Children often tell of these visits. Unfortunately, adults try to convince them that they are wrong, that it is impossible. Adults would be better served to listen to these accounts and remind themselves of Christ's words, "This that I do, you can do also."

Jesus, the Christ, came to model for humanity how to live and how to die. If one is to believe the message of Christ, one must accept that death has no meaning. Still, humanity mourns the passing of the body. It believes there is no hope for returning from the dead. They often fear even to speak of death, as if speaking the words will draw the Grim Reaper to the door. Even the images used to portray death are always dark and foreboding.

Eartheans should celebrate the process of death. Fireworks should be used, to illustrate the joy and release that occurs. A celebration of independence is much more appropriate. Those who pass over celebrate the shedding of the heaviness of the physical. It is a great and wondrous process. Humanity, when fully awakened, will give thanks for the loving lesson that Jesus, the Christ, taught with his life.

Christ taught that life has no beginning or Earthean ending, that life is everlasting. Christ taught that *whatever* humanity believed would come to pass. He taught that wherever an Earthean focused his/her mind, there would be where the treasures of his/her life would be stored. These riches could affect the glory of God's kingdom or be invested in pain and suffering. Christ taught humanity that it had the right to choose its path—and, indeed, its destiny.

Christ willingly chose to be hung on the cross to show humanity a greater world that lay beyond the physical. But all Eartheans could see was the pain and suffering. Jesus was not in pain when he was on the cross, for he could move beyond it.

Just as the Lamaze method currently teaches Earthean women to move beyond the discomfort associated with childbirth, so also as one attunes to the universal love vibration, pain cannot exist. Pain is the result of resistance to the experience.

Christ did not resist. He moved willingly into his role, for he knew humanity needed a model in order to grow. He felt great joy to be finally completing his Earth mission. He was going home successful and triumphant. He felt no suffering or shame, for that would have come from judgment and resistance. He was, indeed, joyful. He was also wise enough to realize that had he expressed this joy while hanging on the cross, he would have been labeled insane; therefore, he played the part of a poor, tortured, dying man to satisfy all those present that he was, indeed, an ordinary Earthean like any other.

Jesus was born a mortal man; therefore he, too, had a veil placed at birth to block his remembrance. He, too, had to struggle with trust in the unknown Divine plan. He, too, had to surrender to God's will. When he had accomplished this, he became Jesus, the Christ, savior of the world. His veil was lifted, slowly at first, just as it occurs for modern Eartheans.[1] Finally, when his tests and trials were complete, he was given total knowing. This full awakening included full knowledge of his real mission on Earth, which was *the crucifixion and resurrection.*

Christ understood, after all, that anyone could have walked around teaching love and brotherhood. Many then did, as many do now. They receive little attention. If *teaching* had been his mission, he would have tried to draw the biggest crowds possible to hear his lessons. Instead, Jesus was content talking to whoever was present.

[1] *Many of the Earth-based volunteers who are entering the physical now as children will be the bridge builders for the New Day on Terra. They have not had a veil placed over their remembrance nor been enveloped with the inability to see beyond the physical dimension. They may well speak of their friends on the other side. They may well speak of other Earthean walks taken. They may speak of friends who visit from other dimensions. These children have chosen special parents who assist and protect them from a well-meaning but confused world. Listen to their words, for they know that of which they speak. The time is short and their job is important; no time is allowed for their awakening.*

A new group of children, more powerful than we can imagine, are scheduled for Earth entry very shortly. These children will be born to special mothers who carry a very high vibration. The mothers may even be beyond the child-bearing years and may not conceive in the traditional way. These children will remain with their family for a very short while—perhaps five or six years—before going off to live together in small clusters to raise themselves. This is necessary to prevent contamination from humanity's limiting beliefs.

If you know of such children and wish to share your knowledge, please write to Dr. Heather Anne Harder, c/o Light Publishing, 210 So. Main St., Crown Point, IN 46307. Please indicate whether or not you would allow your account to be published.

If teaching had been his main mission, he would have left volumes of carefully worded lessons. Instead, Jesus chose to destroy all of his own written material. He knew that anything written would have become mere rigid dogma, just rules to follow. He did not want that. Instead of written lessons, he left the unwritten legacy of his life, a model for others to follow.

Jesus' sojourn left us a story of an ordinary Earthean man who loved all things, a man who always had time for the rich, the poor, the sick, the loyal follower, as well as the enemy—a man who lived the life of love and spoke of its virtue.

No, Jesus did not come to be a teacher, even though he did teach. He knew his loyal followers who would come after him would be the real teachers. He knew his life mission was to show Eartheans for centuries to come that it was time to free themselves of the thoughts of pain, suffering, limitation, and death. After all, teaching is an honorable profession, but it lacks the history-making impact of a well-attended, public crucifixion/resurrection.

Christ was not disappointed in the crucifixion. He knew the Divine plan was perfect. He knew a public execution was needed in order to show the world that he was truly dead. He was not dying for sin. He was dying to set people free—truly free—of pain, suffering, limitation, and death. Jesus was dying to allow humanity to see how to free themselves from their thoughts of limitation and how to accept the heavenly gifts of love, joy, and abundance.

Christ said, "Forgive them, for they know not what they do," not to God, but to all those who would hear. Jesus knew God's plan was perfect, and he knew that God was aware of this perfection. Jesus also knew that the men and women responsible for his crucifixion were only players in this grand proceeding and, at a conscious level, they did not know what they were doing. He uttered these words for the multitude who were in attendance or who would later hear or read about his crucifixion, and feel anger, hate, or guilt, as a result.

It was a final, supreme example of forgiveness for all to learn. It was as much for the Eartheans of today as for those of his time that Christ uttered those immortalized last words.

Jesus did not suffer, because suffering and pain exist only in the minds of humans. Christ had moved beyond concerns of the physical. Christ played a part that allowed those responsible to *feel* they had caused suffering and pain and eventually death, but, in truth, no one can inflict these things on another except to the extent they are allowed.

Jesus, the Christ, son of God and brother to all humanity, had been called to volunteer on behalf of Mother Earth. He had heard God's call and lovingly came to serve his Earthean family. He had accomplished all that had been asked and he had done it well.

Lord Sananda, one of the many special Earth-based volunteers, had completed his mission. Now the rest was up to humanity and other Earth-based volunteers. Eartheans again had to choose, and choose they did.

Eartheans chose to make Jesus into an Earthean idol, as they forgot his ideas. Jesus came to bring love to the planets; humanity fought wars in his behalf. He came in the name of unity for all Eartheans, but, instead, Eartheans have used his name and life as a reason to divide, kill, and maim. There are over four hundred religions that claim to follow Jesus, the Christ, yet many openly condemn the others.

Jesus came with a message but was made a messiah. Jesus came to show all Eartheans that they are the children of the God Force, worthy of all and great in their own right. Instead, humanity chose to believe it not. But still, the fuse had been lit. The process had been started. The rest was up to humanity.

One man could be stopped, but not easily, as seen in the teachings of Christ. But the second coming, as Jesus promised, would happen.

The second coming would not be Lord Sananda entering again into physical embodiment, but all the Earth-based volunteers moving into their Christhood. Jesus had shown the way. He had demonstrated the powers and the wisdom that come with this Divine attainment. He lit the way for the many volunteers to follow.

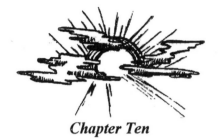

Chapter Ten

The Awakening

esus, the Christ, had served humanity well, for he reminded all of love. The brutality of his passing was sharply contrasted with the gentle, good-natured, love-filled life he led. The contrast was everlasting. Jesus served both Eartheans and the Earth-based volunteers, for he had begun the awakening process. *Once one operates in the vibrational frequency of love, all else is made known.* The Divine frequency ensures that the volunteer has access to all awareness and knowledge.

Jesus caused humanity to become conscious of its heritage of love and perfect peace. This was and is, indeed, the process of awakening.

The awakening was gentle at first, designed to remind all those in residence on Earth that love is the answer to all questions, problems, challenges, and life circumstances. When love was desired and recognized, the turning inward was easy, for humanity would again begin to resonate to the universal love vibration.

Eartheans would again willingly turn inward to hear God's message and feel the Oneness with All-That-Is. Once Eartheans were aware of their connectedness to the Divine, then more of their energies can be directed, aligned with the powerful force of love. This would allow many more Eartheans to grow beyond previous Earthean limitations. And from this growth, still others would grow. This was the plan for awakening humanity. This ever-widening influence acts much like a pebble cast into a pond, causing an ever-expanding disturbance in the water.

The awakening process can occur in several ways. It can occur naturally, over time, or abruptly. The spiritual forces can act much like a parent who lets the children sleep until awakening on their own, or more like a parent who, upon hearing the alarm, goes in to gently, lovingly awaken the sleeping children. Now, as then, is the time of awakening on Mother Earth, but how it occurs is unique to the individual.

Over eons of time, God had allowed humanity to awaken on its own. However, time was running short for Mother Earth, so God had sent Jesus (and many other obedient messengers) to sound the alarm. Jesus had done his task well, as had many before and after him. It was time now for those who desired to assist with the preparation for the new day on Terra to arise. Mother Earth was in need.

This awakening process continues. Those who wish to help must rise, wipe their eyes, and proceed. As it was then, so it is now.

Those of Earth who wish to help with this great Earth transformation must not worry about the paths of others. They must stay focused upon their own path and not be concerned about those who may continue to sleep. They must not concern themselves with those who appear to be far ahead of them on the Divine path, as this causes them to judge and compare, which serves no one.

Those who wish to assist must rise and get about God's business. The activity and vibrational changes of the workers of light may awaken the sleepers, but if that does not happen, that, too, is O.K. Free will gives each the right of choice. *Eartheans may choose not to awaken. The transformation will occur nonetheless.* The absence of judgment will cause it to be more tranquil. Each Earth-based volunteer will awaken in her/his own way and time.

The way will be disclosed at every step for those who desire to awaken. This does not override free will, for the path is merely shown. God does not wish to work with those without the desire for cooperation. Those who desire to follow the light must take the steps. Through love, trust, and surrender to a higher purpose, one indicates a desire to follow the Divine path.

It is like a giant spiral. When you take the steps, assistance is given over any real or perceived obstacles. When you become stronger in your desire to follow the Radiant One, the way, the purpose, and the Divine plan are made clear.

Over the eons of time of the birth-death-rebirth cycle, the Earth-based volunteers had only to awaken to love, the Divine, universal vibration. As they were able to do this, they assisted others to also raise their vibrational frequency. Often there were special tasks that each was to accomplish in those lifetimes, but usually these were secondary in importance. *The primary goal has been to learn to function and return to God's love while in the Earthean vibrations.*

Now—in this moment, this lifetime—and for the first time in Earthean history, this is not true. Awakening to love is now taken for granted, because it is necessary for the accomplishment of the Earthean mission, which each volunteer agreed to at that glorious conclave.

In this lifetime, it is the mission that is vital to the success and health of Mother Earth. All volunteers must now get about God's business, as they agreed to do long ago.

The great mission and specific tasks that were given to the chosen ones during the Great Conclave eons ago are now of primary importance. The chosen ones must awaken to their mission and to the great need of love on Mother Earth. The healing vibration of love must radiate forth from all of the Earth-based volunteers as the new day is birthed on Terra.

This is a time of birth. The volunteers are on the planet to assist in the birthing of a new day on the Earth Mother. She has carried the burdens of the human race and felt the humiliation of abuse. Now is the time when the consciousness of this planet will become aware of her greatness and the totality of the Oneness of all creation. This is the time of bringing into life a vibrational unity that will connect humanity to the Divine and separation will meld into unity.

This time heralds the birthing of the new vibrational alignment with all our brothers and sisters of the universe. Mother Earth shall no longer be in quarantine, kept separate from her family because of the actions of the Eartheans. This time heralds the anchoring of the heavenly vibration to Terra and of a way of life on Earth full of joy and harmony. This is a time that has been called for with each utterance of the Lord's prayer: *"Your kingdom come, Your will be done, on Earth as it is in heaven."*

In any birth process, there is a time of labor. This period is not always comfortable. It is a time of going from one state of beingness into another. One must give up the old to move into the new. It may even be a time of discomfort and pain. The period can be relatively brief, or longer in duration. It can be a time of great anticipation for what is to come, or it can be one of pain, for those who hold on and resist the process.

The great time of transition is upon Mother Earth. Now the loving legions of light workers who volunteered to come to Earth must awaken to their great assignment. They are to act as a midwife through the birthing process of the new day.

Their awakening to the loving God Essence is necessary, and as this happens, the greater knowing will occur. The truth will be self-evident. These volunteers will begin to have remembrances of past lives spent in service on Terra. They may have a strange, compelling need to follow a direction or take an action. This they may or may not understand. They will begin to have a closeness with the God Force through prayer, meditation, and communication that few will understand.

Diets will change in order to prepare the physical body for the higher frequencies. More water will be consumed. Interests and friends will change. *Love will come to be the basis for all action.*

If you feel you are one of the awakening ones, you, too, may be drawn to new places, people, things, and events. *Trust your feelings and follow your inner guidance.* It may not always make sense, but it will always bring a sense of joy and self-satisfaction, for these are the Divine whisperings of the God Source.

Some volunteers may be drawn to special stones, crystals, colors, tones, and music. All of these have different vibrational frequencies and each will bring to the personal frequency what is needed for the higher vibration.

Trust will be the key. Learning to trust in the power of self, learning to trust the Divine connection and one's inner guidance concerning these matters, will be a challenge for many Eartheans. *Learning to trust one's worthiness to interact with the Divine Force will be a challenge.*

These changes will assist in harmonizing the personal and planetary frequencies to the frequencies of the God Source. In the end, volunteers must listen only to their inner guidance, and not the external guidance of a well-meaning friend, teacher, or sales clerk.

Each and every change will be individually prescribed, based on needs, as dictated by the higher self, in conjunction with the God Essence. These changes cannot be rushed, but they can be slowed.

By listening and responding to inner guidance, the process is facilitated. *Taking the time to go to center and heed the inner guid-*

ance is the key. Resist not the love and light, and the transformation shall be swift and harmonious.

Each Earthean resident has free will; therefore, each will choose his/her individual path and rate of progress. Listen not to those who say what to do and how to proceed. They know not the individual path. Go within, and there each will receive instructions, confirmations, and wisdom. The wee, small voice can be heard by all who will but listen and trust.

A Letter from the God Force to the Earth-Based Volunteers

Dear Child of God,

Many of you wish to know the mission, the time, and the date, for these Earth details are often considered important. They are impossible to give, as free will allows Eartheans to determine them.

If enough love could be felt in the hearts of humanity, then paradise could be achieved tomorrow. This is not likely, since humanity has encrusted itself in so much judgment, hate, fear, and self-concern. If the entire mission were disclosed, with all the possible alternatives, it would cause the mortal mind and body to run with fear, for Eartheans would see themselves as unworthy of such wondrous acts.

Dear ones, you have held yourselves back so long with these thoughts of limitation. You call it humility, but truly it is not. Humility is simply the awareness of everyone's greatness, and no need is present to demonstrate your greatness over another. Instead, these thoughts of your own limitations act as a shield and an excuse not to take action on the physical, mental, and spiritual levels. Thus, if one feels oneself incapable, then acts and fails, it is not one's "fault," because one was incapable. Or if one fails to take action when knowing oneself to be incapable, wisdom would be claimed, for action would have brought failure.

When one knows of one's greatness as a child of God, accepts that greatness, and feels the call to action, then one steps forward into service, knowing that victory is the only outcome. One is then aligned with God, and God is always victorious.

Starting with the love essence is the first step. Develop that vibration, for when one is truly living in the God Essence, also called love, then one must act and move in harmony with Divine will. You will be called to take action first in small ways, then in larger ones. You will be successful when you maintain the love. When you forget and move into fear, anger, self-concern, or any other vibrations that are not in harmony with love, you will be unable to fulfill the calling.

The calling will be different for each person. Each must listen and heed the wee, small, inner voice. There will be no mistaking the calling. Each will recognize it as truth. Then each must decide whether or not to step out in faith. The choice will not always be easy, but free will allows each the right to choose and then follow that choice. These small steps shall build confidence in listening to and following the Divine inner guidance.

You are each important to the Earth mission. Truly you have each chosen an important role. This was done eons ago, not merely in this lifetime. This process of preparation and readiness has occurred over many lifetimes. Now is the time you must reawaken your memory of this process and your role. As you do this, you must accept your own greatness, for great you are.

Much love has been poured over you, infused into you, exchanged with you, for through love you can feel your connectedness to your Source. You will realize your own ability to co-create. When this happens on a regular basis, you will have chosen to accept the greatness of all. The vibrations of Earth shall soar. Your mission will have been accomplished.

Blessings from the Source from which all blessings flow.

Chapter Eleven

Removing the Veil

eawakening the memory of the Earth mission is an important task for the Earthean volunteers. This process has been referred to as removing the veil. *The veil is the invisible separation between physical existence and other dimensions. This veil also separates humanity from the memory of All-That-Is.* It allows humans to think that their life is independent of other God Force creations. The veil is what causes humanity to feel that, in all of the universe, they, alone, are the only intelligent, living beings. This wasn't always the way it was on Earth.

Humanity once had the ability to see and hear those of different dimensions. As Eartheans encountered these beings, they often thought them to be gods. They began to worship these visitors instead of trying to reunite with the one, true, God Force. The more the Eartheans worshipped these beings, the more difficult it became to reconnect with the Radiant One.

They saw these new "gods" as a means of great wealth and other abundance that a god could provide. These new gods had come from the heavens, and humanity knew this to be the residence of the God Force. Like humans originally could, many of these dimensional beings had the ability to manifest physical form into anything desired. This excited Eartheans, who had lost this ability. They worshipped the gifted visitors as gods, though they were not.

Many brothers and sisters from the heavens came to visit Earth. It was, after all, unique in all the universe. Some visitors came to Earth to be of service to the God Force, others to satisfy their curiosity, still others to study physical existence, and a few for personal gain.

The vast majority of these visitors from space tried to help Eartheans; therefore, they refused to allow humans to worship them. These visitors, instead, tried to teach Eartheans about their own abilities and the source of all abilities. Sometimes the Eartheans would listen and sometimes not.

The visitors who came for personal gain rather enjoyed being gods, so they allowed and even encouraged, "those silly Earth creatures to act so foolishly." Humanity became willing servants to what they perceived as great ones. Eartheans had to have a god. If they could not reconnect to the only, true, God Force, then any god would do. For they still had the memory of this connection etched in their subconscious mind and they longed to experience it once again.

The visitors to Earth who were attempting to help humanity were upset with the ones who attempted to take advantage of the Eartheans. They asked for intervention on behalf of humanity. Thus, the veil was placed over the perception of humanity, limiting the Eartheans' perceptions of those of different frequencies. This veil allowed Eartheans to be influenced only by their own kind—those who shared a similar vibrational existence.

Earth and the Eartheans had been placed in a planetary state of isolation. Eartheans were no longer able to co-exist with the heavenly siblings. It was felt that, for Earth's own good, it should no longer have open contact with other members of the universe.

No longer could they worship the visitors from space, because they could no longer perceive them. However, free will was still the law. Therefore, if the Eartheans asked for or raised their vibration significantly to achieve this awareness, they could pierce the veil and the illusion that they were the only intelligent creations of the God Force.

Eartheans could again become aware of the higher dimensions that were their destiny. The choice was still theirs.

The veil caused a separation in consciousness between Eartheans and the many other planets, universes, and life forms. This was a quarantine of sorts, but needed, if humanity was to learn to once again turn toward the God Source for direction and inspiration.

But now it is time once again for Eartheans to take their place in the family of God. The veil is being thinned, in preparation for its removal.

The space brothers and sisters who were concerned for the well-being of the Earth and Eartheans did not vacate the planet simply because they were no longer seen. Most found new ways to serve the Living Light and Mother Earth, because they cared not if they were noticed or appreciated.

Some dimensional beings took on animal forms, for they could lower their vibrations, thus allowing Earthean perception. As animals, these visitors could again reawaken humanity to the love that was its salvation. As animals, they could also closely monitor Earthean progress without interference. They could assist, yet not disturb, Divine will. They were also still free from the karmic cycle on Earth. They could/would not get entrapped by the Earthean world of illusion.

Think of the creatures of Earth. Think now of the ones that cause your heart to sing and resonate to love and joy. Think of the ones who remind you of God's beauty and wisdom. Many on Terra recognize the specialness of the dolphins and whales but miss the Divine Intelligence found in the more common creatures. Could these be brothers and sisters from other dimensions?

Some space friends chose to maintain their own life form and assist from their own dimension. They could not influence people directly because that was forbidden, but they could assist humanity indirectly. They chose to stand guard in the sky and protect the Earth from the lower-vibrational energy rays. They serve to keep the frequencies in harmony and balance.

These alien friends have always been with Earth. They play many roles. They assist in stabilizing the Earth and helping humanity through Earthly challenges and natural disasters. In these disaster situations, they may remove and then replace Eartheans in the twinkling of an eye, always by Earthean invitation. Eartheans later tell how, by the grace of God, they were saved. Truly this is correct, for these friends do radiate the grace of God.

These alien volunteers stand ever ready to share light and love with Earth and the Eartheans. They, too, are members of the light family, but they choose not to enter into physical existence, feeling they can make a more important contribution to the well-being of Earth in their own way.

These alien friends will often communicate when there is an Earthean desire to do so and when it serves the greater purpose. They have much to share with humanity. Always their goal is to bring Eartheans into higher vibrations so all can radiate the love vibration.

When there is desire and need on the part of humanity, the alien crafts can be seen. This is possible because the space brothers and sisters have the ability to lower the vibrational frequency of themselves and their crafts for a period of time, making them visible to the human eye.

Earth-based volunteers often dream of being on-board spacecraft. These are not dreams, but, rather, remembrances of nonphysical visits for the purpose of instruction and/or preparation.

As Eartheans and the Earth-based volunteers raise their vibrations, more and more contacts are being made. As each vibrational rate becomes stabilized at a higher level, Eartheans no longer tremble with fear when they see the spacecrafts emerge from the clouds, as fear is the last thing these light workers wish to induce. As greater numbers of Eartheans are at peace with the idea of having alien assistance, then many more friends from other dimensions will become apparent.

But Eartheans need to be aware that not all space brothers and sisters are working for the light and love of the Radiant One. Some, like people on Earth, work for personal power and control. Humanity must be ever on the guard against these, for they, too, can and do influence humanity, with less-than-positive results.

Asking the God Source for the gift of discernment is all that is needed, for what is asked for is given. *Discernment gives the power of determining what is of the highest light and what is not.* Discernment allows Eartheans to separate truth from illusion, sincerity from fraud, and God's will from personal motive.

The aliens fall into two broad categories—those who work on behalf of the light and those who do not. Those who work on behalf of the light dedicate their existence to serving the God Essence. Those who do not serve the light choose to serve personal needs and desires. They are referred to as "those of lesser light." It is not meant as a judgment, but as a term of recognition.

Those who are of the light recognize their unity with All-That-Is; therefore, they serve the greater whole. Those who serve the light are always in tune with the God Source and follow the will of God.

They take action based on Divine guidance and not personal gain. They recognize that all are one and what affects one affects all.

Those of lesser light fail to recognize their unity with All-That-Is; therefore, they serve their own needs above all others. Those of lesser light may be well-intentioned and truly feel that they can solve many of the problems that humanity faces. They choose to make the decisions for Eartheans, thereby violating the free will of others. *They feel it is best to do unto others before they can do it to them.* They can take control only when Eartheans allow, cooperate, or surrender their free will; however, Eartheans are usually quick to surrender their precious gift of free will.

Again be reminded that the lesser lights are easy to recognize if you but go within and ask for discernment, then trust the inner knowing. The lesser lights can be very tricky and deceptive, so it is wise to always ask for discernment. *Feel their vibrations.* Do they radiate the love and light of the God Force? *Listen to their words.* Are they giving you a cookbook approach to all that you desire?

A sure sign of a lesser light is the amount of control they wish to have over others. They feel *they* know the best answers and the best plan of actions; therefore, they will tell humanity what to do and say. They never honor free will and the Earthean's divinely given right to make choices and even mistakes. The lesser lights do not wish you harm. They, like a well-meaning parent who wishes to dictate the actions of his/her adult child, refuse to honor the unique life choice of the Eartheans. So, too, do these lesser-light beings feel they are serving the planet. Be ever aware that *no one serves the Earth Mother by violating the heart of her nature.* Free will is the nature and the very heart of this planet and must be honored by all, regardless of the circumstance or possible outcome.

An alien who serves God will give you alternatives and warn of the possible outcomes of your actions, but will always suggest that you go within and listen to your God Source, which, alone, knows your best path. Those working on behalf of the Living Light will always build your confidence in your inner guidance and connection to the God Source.

If you should have an encounter with an alien or a nonphysical being and you are not sure of the alien's intention, there are many things you can do. It is wise to remember that *you are in charge and you must be obeyed.*

If you are in doubt of their motivational source, just ask. *All things and all beings are from the one God Source, but not all use this same God Source as a motivation for their actions.* Those who come in light and love will always tell you that they come in light and love because they wear that vibration as a badge of honor.

Those who do not come in light and love cannot lie, as it is forbidden by universal Law. So when you ask "Do you come in light and love?" they must answer truthfully. They can, however, ignore the question, responding with another question (like "Why are you asking that? Don't you know who I am?" etc.), and they can change the topic or otherwise evade your question. These behaviors are allowed, as they are not direct lies. So be ever aware of trickery and evasion. Those of lesser light are very skilled at it.

Your best choice in this situation is to keep repeating the question. If they have not given you a straight answer by the third time you ask the question, then, no matter how helpful they seem or how many gifts they bear, send them away with light and love. Sample wording might be *"If you do not come in light and love, then you are to leave me immediately and you are never to return."* Repeat this three times, as there is great power in three.

You have the power to send them away and they must obey you because you have chosen to operate in the physical world and they have not. This is your *right*, for it is *your world*. You do not need to entertain beings who are not for your highest and best good. *They must obey you*, for it is *your free will* that is allowed on Earth. They can influence you only if you allow. Because of their ability to manifest what is wanted by the Eartheans, some on Earth now cooperate with aliens of lesser light. (The risks far outweigh any possible benefits.)

Sometimes their influence can be perceived as help because they meet our most basic needs. There was a story in a magazine about a small European town that was visited by aliens. At first those in town were frightened of their presence. Then the aliens proceeded to heal all people who were sick. The people rejoiced. Then the aliens showed the residents how to heal the sick. So the residents of this town cured anyone and everyone they could think of, and so it went. The people of this town were given everything they needed. Their benevolent aliens worked hand in hand with the people, or so it seemed. Who do you think made decisions and controlled the town? Only those who allow it can be controlled.

Assuming the story is true, it brings to mind the tale of a New England fishing village. The fish processing plant in this little village would throw all the scraps to the pelicans rather than waste them. The pelicans enjoyed the treat. But eventually the fishing market dried up and the plant closed. The people were amazed when the pelicans began to starve. It seems the pelicans had forgotten how to fish for their own food and had become dependent upon the scraps. Now they were dying as a result of this dependency. A smart villager thought to add some wild pelicans to the dependent pelicans and sure enough, it worked. The wild pelicans went out each morning to fish and the dependent ones eventually followed and learned again how to fish for themselves. (Does this story remind you about the entry of the Earth-based volunteers to this dear Planet?)

A person or group of people who take care of all your needs will cause dependency. Dependency leads to surrender of control. Life may become challenging at times, but as long as Eartheans scratch for their own existence, they are independent and in control of their own fate.

One person who resists that control can often teach others how to break the chains. Behaviors leading to control are seductive, enticing others to give up their free will. It is far more effective than war and violence because people are given trivial choices to lead them to believe they retain control.

The aliens in the European town are training the residents to be dependent on an outside source rather than rely on their own abilities. They may or may not have ulterior motives and less-than-honorable intentions. It matters not, for the outcome will be the same. These people are being controlled and manipulated by others.

These aliens stepped in and healed the residents apparently without being asked or receiving permission. That is interference and is in violation of free will. It is sometimes hard to accept that illness serves humanity, but it does. Illness can cause great growth and wisdom, and it is always the choice of the sick person, either consciously, subconsciously, or at a higher level of consciousness. Sickness can also be a result of choices made while on Earth. Only an alien of lesser light would step into a physical world and alter Earthean choice without being asked to do so.

When the man Jesus walked this Earth, he had the power to heal. But he healed only those who came to him and asked or when a parent of a child under age thirteen asked on behalf of the child. He could have healed *all* leprosy, blindness, and other such burdens of the day, but he did not. He respected and honored free will.

Dependency and the abdication of free will are the eventual outcomes of a relationship with beings of lesser light. Their only desire is to control and manipulate your thoughts, words, and actions. Sometimes they feel they can help humanity more this way and sometimes it is because they desire to control, but always the outcome is the same. Beware of anything or anyone who wishes to tell you what to do or say and nibbles away at your free will.

Once the aliens of lesser light are in cooperation, the Eartheans often fear breaking away from them, feeling trapped and helpless. Guilt keeps them from turning to the God Force for assistance, but these Eartheans have nothing to fear, for God has freely given them choice.

All they must do is choose to work in harmony with the Divine will, which is always in harmony with light and love. Many governmental leaders are trapped today because of the fear of breaking away and the fear of public opinion if their relationship with those of lesser light were made known.

The lesser lights encourage Eartheans to judge, because they know it is a powerful tool for control. When attempts are made to break away from the lesser lights, Eartheans are threatened with scandal. The fear of public judgment keeps them subdued even when it is not in their best interest. As those on Mother Earth turn away from fear and judgment, these tools of control will become useless. As the Eartheans turn to unconditional love and acceptance of the path of others, the more all will be able to stand in their personal power, free from the control of others.

Eartheans can ask for Divine protection from these alien forces, and visualize themselves and all of Earth surrounded by the radiant light of the Divine Intelligence. This will act as a shield against anything that the aliens of lesser light could do.

No power exists that can match the power of God. *Fear not,* for fear opens the door to these lower vibrations. *Fear allows those of lesser light to penetrate the light.* Those who desire the light must know that by fearing, they have chosen to cooperate with the lesser lights. But it is the Earthean's God-given right to choose again, to co-operate only with the most Divine, most loving Source of all.

A space brother or sister who is working on behalf of the God Essence will applaud this decision to work only for the light and love of God. A space brother or sister working on behalf of their own gain will curse, condemn, ridicule, threaten, or try to persuade you not to change your choice. *Remember, the choice is yours. All must allow your choice to prevail.* And just as the loving father waited with out-spread arms for the prodigal son, so, too, does the God Force wait for those who, in their past, have chosen to work cooperatively with the lesser lights.

The Earth-based volunteers have come from many universes to serve Mother Earth and the God Force. So, too, have their brothers and sisters of space. This heavenly body of beings guards the skies on behalf of Mother Earth and the Creator of All-That-Is. These beings have chosen to act as the messengers of the God Essence. These heav-enly guardians of other dimensions have been given many names through-out Earthean history, though they are most often referred to as angelic hosts or angels.

If those of Earth could but send love and open their hearts to the truth, the veil would be discarded, and we at last could meet our heavenly guardians. The family of God would once again be united.

Alas, as long as fear and judgment are humanity's response, our heavenly helpers shall remain cloaked in the clouds, hidden by the stars, and waiting for Eartheans to open their hearts to the truth of All-That-Is.

The Earth-based volunteers have given up their connection with the Oneness in order to serve the God Force and Mother Earth. They willingly chose to enter and reenter the Earth's vibrations to show humanity how to lift themselves into the loving arms of the waiting God Presence. These volunteers continue to work, for the hour is near when they shall complete their Earthean responsibility and again return home—home to a vibrational existence at one with all All-That-Is. No longer will Mother Earth be plagued with a world divided by good and bad, me and you, us and them, right and wrong. The world of duality will give way to a world of unity.

A hero's welcome awaits the volunteers who work on behalf of Terra. But now, they face the most demanding aspect of their mission. They must fully awaken to their specific task, and then, with loving hearts, complete their mission.

All of the Earth-based volunteers feel some hesitation and trepidation, for most have experienced ridicule, failure, torture, and even death, in past lives, as the result of unknowing Eartheans who labeled them heretics, zealots, and lunatics. Still, they move forward to the front lines to take their place in the history books of planet Earth. They shall prepare the Earthean vibrations for a smooth, loving transition to a new day—or else assist humanity to see the loving, wondrous perfection in the not-so-smooth process of Earth's purification.

Either way, they shall assist Eartheans to feel joy and love in their hearts when destruction and chaos meet the eye. They shall open the hearts and minds of humanity to a much vaster universe than it is now ready to accept.

In its infancy, humanity felt that the universe was anything it could touch. As the infant grew to toddlerhood, its universe opened to all that could be seen and reached. As the toddler grew, its world expanded to include the house, then the neighborhood, then the block, then the school and community. Finally, an awareness of the nation and the world was formed, even though they could not be immediately seen.

For the first time in known history, the current Eartheans have viewed Earth from afar, via space satellites. Now the time is here for humanity to finally recognize that the universe is, indeed, vast, and Earth and Eartheans are but one small aspect of it. It is time to know and accept that there are universes beyond universes that contain intelligent life forms now eagerly awaiting the Earthean changes. It is time for Earth and humanity to again learn to live in harmony with All-That-Is. It is time for humanity to reunite with its heavenly family.

All of the Earth-based volunteers know the hour is close, for they feel an urgency, even though they may not understand these feelings. The volunteers who have already awakened to the mission are sounding the alarm for all Eartheans and their fellow volunteers to rise and get about God's business.

Chapter Twelve

Understanding the Nature of Mother Earth

Jn order to share Mother Earth's perspective on the Earth mission and the Earth-based volunteers, the volunteers must first understand the nature of Earth herself. They do, of course, in an off-planet state, but not while wearing the Earthean vibration. To fully understand Earth, one must first understand the nature of the various dimensions.

The term *dimension* is used frequently on Earth, even though few who use the word truly understand it. This was an intentional process. The Earthean world is defined and controlled with words; therefore, the vocabulary must often be introduced to the planet before full understanding of the word is achieved.

This awareness and understanding of the dimensions first begins with the most familiar—the third dimension—and continues to those that are more difficult to comprehend. (These dimensions are discussed at greater length in one of my other books, *Perfect Power in Consciousness*).

First you must grasp the concept of dimension. *The dimension is a state of being*, an orientation of sorts to all life experiences. Each dimension carries with it a vibrational frequency range that carries an underlying reality that greatly affects the way beings perceive their experiences.

Using the theater as a metaphor for life on Earth, the dimension is the temperature, lighting, and air quality within the building, not the scenery or script.

If the actor is in a well-lit, well-ventilated, and comfortable environment, then he/she will greatly enjoy the drama, whether it is a country or city scene, or whether playing a poor peasant or a rich and handsome leading character. If the reverse is true—if it is too hot or too cold or if the air is unpleasant—then the actor will find little joy, no matter what the scene or role played. His/her misery would detract from whatever the actor happens to be playing. More than likely, the actor would continue with this part, but his/her joy and comfort would be greatly affected.

As this illustrates, a dimensional state is not a place nor a physical state, as some people believe. People often say, "I live in the third dimension" or "I live in a third-dimensional world." In truth, dimensions are not a place or a location but, rather, the perspective or attitude from which one views one's life experiences.

Each dimension has a frequency range—the higher the frequency, the higher the dimension. *Frequency limits or expands one's perception.* The higher the frequency, the more encompassing the perception. The higher the frequency and, thus, the dimensional state, the more joy and freedom found in any life circumstance. The higher the frequency, the more love and light one allows in one's life.

All frequencies and dimensional states provide opportunity for growth. Existence in any life form is all about growth. Lessons are forever. One dimension is not better or worse than another, just as kindergarten is neither better nor worse than first grade. They are just different; therefore, they afford unique experiences and allow different lessons. One must go through one level to be ready for the next.

Remember the old 3-D glasses handed out during certain movies? You could watch the movie without the glasses, but when you put the glasses on and viewed the movie through that simple paper and plastic apparatus, it changed. It was the same movie but a new experience, with greater depth and realism. So it is with dimensions. Each is unique and gives its own particular experiences.

Third Dimension

Until recently, most Eartheans existed in the third dimension. This is characterized by the basic physical perceptions. In the third dimension you believe that what is real (and thus important) is what you can see, hear, taste, smell, and touch. Your physical senses dictate what is real. You have a "real" physical life filled with sensations and input given to you through these senses. Your beliefs are formed as a result of your experiences. You see life through what is perceived through your physical eyes. Words spoken often determine your personal mood. This is the most basic third-dimensional reality.

In third-dimensional reality, everything that you can touch, taste, smell, see, and hear is real, but nothing else. Things you cannot touch, taste, smell, see, or hear are not real to you. If I told a third-dimensional reality-based person about how angels are helping all those who will allow it, he/she might well laugh or want to lock me away because that person would *know* angels are not real. And if I told that same person that someone could read his/her mind, he/she would not believe it because mind reading is silly or evil, from that person's perspective.

At the most basic level of third-dimensional consciousness, one sees oneself as a victim of life, helpless to influence it in even the most basic ways. One believes that one merely functions and survives. For those who are at this level, it may not be a very fun place to be. They see themselves as a feather being blown about on the winds of life. They feel they are victims of everyone else's reality.

Most people functioning at this level do not believe in the existence of God because there is no *proof* that *"He"* exists. Until they get proof, they cannot believe. A little higher on this third-dimension frequency scale would be the third-dimensional people who accept God's existence.

This God is patterned after their reality; therefore, God is a humanlike being who punishes the bad and rewards the good. This God punishes them when they do something wrong and rewards them when they do something right. ("I did something wrong; therefore, God burned my house down." "I was kind to an old lady, so God allowed me to win the lottery.") They see poverty as a result of a person's bad deeds and abundance as God's reward. This concept of God is dictated by their third-dimensional reality. Therefore, God exists as a person-type being who lives in heaven, a wonderful place to visit, somewhere just beyond the stars (take a left at Saturn), but you have to die first. If you screw up in life, you go to hell (take a right at Saturn, and take plenty of water).

At the highest level of the third dimension, one would begin to release the need to have a person-type God and allow a greater variety of form. One would begin to see God as the Creator of diversity and, therefore, diverse in Its own existence. But God is still separate from that person in third dimension. "I am here and God is in heaven." *It is the separateness that earmarks the third dimension and third-dimensional reality.*

At the outermost reaches of a third-dimensional frequency, a slight awareness emerges of a reality greater than the five senses can perceive. At this level, Eartheans become curious about some of the things that can't be seen, tasted, touched, heard, or smelled—like astrology or psychic phenomena. (At the most basic third-dimensional level, all of these would be ridiculed or condemned.) As the dimensional reality shifts, one might begin to read the astrology section of the paper for entertainment, (but it wouldn't be believed) or a psychic might be visited, just for the fun of it.

Fourth Dimension

As the vibrational frequency is increased, so, too, is the dimensional reality that is perceived. At the fourth dimension, Eartheans begin to recognize the control they have over their lives and take a little more responsibility for their world.

They become aware that they are not a victim of life, but are living in a cause-and-effect world. As Eartheans become aware that they are responsible for their world, this can be a little scary. (Many fourth-dimensional thinkers retreat to the safety and security of the *real*, or third-dimensional, world at this point.) There, in the security of the third dimension, one does not assume responsibility, but can blame the rest of the world for one's life challenges.

Often Eartheans expect great changes as they move into the fourth dimension, but it doesn't happen like that. It is simply a gradual awakening to the possibility (and finally the reality) that there is more

> The fourth dimension is very complicated for the mortal mind to grasp. It is what Eartheans experience in the dream state. It is a dimension beyond the physical; it is of the energy spirits. It is the hearing of what is not there. It is knowing what can't be known. It is what many can already do, but trust it not because it is not "normal." But soon it will be normal. Now is the time of a great awakening to the vastness of life. It will be a moving beyond the limits of the physical. It is knowing the joy of the angels. It is recognizing your Oneness with All-That-Is. It is a glorious time. Let us pray and send light and love that those others of Earth shall move into it without struggle or resistance.

to this life than can be seen, heard, smelled, touched, and tasted. No lightning bolts from heaven or major life adjustments occur. The fourth dimension is not "out there," but within the perceptual reality of each Earthean, waiting to emerge.

As Eartheans move into fourth-dimensional reality, they begin to realize that there is something greater than physical existence. They begin to know that there are things that cannot be seen, heard, touched, smelled, or tasted but that exist nevertheless. They realize there is a connection between themselves and other worlds. They begin to search out these other existences. They will find evidence of these other worlds through their channel of perception. The three most common senses through which people find proof are hearing, seeing, and feeling without ears, eyes, or fingers.

Clairaudience is the hearing of sounds, music, and voices not audible to normal hearing. This French term means clear hearing. It is not a new phenomenon. Oracles, priests, mystics, shamen, adepts, saints, prophets, and holy persons through the ages have recorded occurrences of clairaudient experiences. A few decades ago, if people heard voices, they would be locked away, perhaps forever, because they were considered abnormal or insane. Even that was better than being burned at the stake as a witch, which was a typical punishment just a few hundred years ago.

As more stable, intelligent, sincere, and honest Eartheans begin to admit to hearing these disembodied voices, their reality can no longer be denied. Some of these voices, either internal or external, will be accepted as conversations with off-planet beings and/or other dimensional beings.

These voices are clearly distinguishable from Earthean ones. Many well-known Eartheans have heard voices that guided them to greatness. Socrates claimed to be guided by a spirit friend throughout his life. When sentenced to death, he willingly drank the poison because his guide did not advise him to do otherwise. Several Bible characters, including King Solomon, admitted to hearing voices. Joan of Arc led armies to victory by advice of her spirit friends. George Washington was said to decide battle strategies based on visits from his angelic helpers.

Clairvoyants see into other dimensions. Clear seeing, or perceiving objects, events, or people that cannot be perceived by the physical eye, is relatively common. Some people see all the forms outside themselves, whereas others get an internal vision.

For Eartheans, the simplest type of clairvoyance is an internal sight of symbolic images, which must be interpreted. In its highest form, one looks into the various dimensions and sees directly. Many Eartheans have reported different types of clairvoyance. Some tell of being able to see through things like envelopes and walls. Some are able to see disease and illness in the energy field of the body or the aura. Some can see faraway events and/or people. Still others are able to see beyond time and space. All are normal and occur frequently, as the Eartheans move into fourth-dimensional reality.

Clairsentience, or clear sensing, is a nonphysical sense perception. It is feeling the information, through feelings beyond the physical. It may come as a fleeting impression, a brief image, intuition, or a gut reaction. These may register as internal or external impressions. Eartheans experience many forms of clairsentience.

The experience is similar to, yet stronger than, intuition. It can often be described as a *soft* idea, only much stronger and clearer. The more Eartheans attend to this knowing, the stronger and clearer it gets and the more confident and trusting they will become with it.

Clairsentience, clairvoyance, and clairaudience are not skills attached to an on/off switch. They are not an either-you-have-them-or-you-don't experience. Instead, they represent a continuum. All Eartheans have these latent skills. If they recognize and use these extrasensory abilities, they will enhance and expand them.

Things can and do exist beyond what can be seen, touched, heard, tasted, and smelled by the physical body. As Eartheans move into a fourth-dimensional consciousness, they know this as their truth.

In the fourth dimension, Eartheans recognize that life is a play and they are both the playwright and casting director. If a terrible mother or an awful father has been written into their script and they are tired of that, they know they have the ability to rewrite it. By changing themselves, they know they have the power to change everything.

No longer can Eartheans say, "Oh, poor me; I just don't have any money this week" or "I don't have..." Instead they ask, "Why did I do that to myself? What is the lesson for me?" When someone really terrible comes into their life, they ask themselves, "What is he/she trying to teach me?"

Third-dimensional reality is fear- and separation-based, whereas fourth dimension is love- and unity-based. Eartheans recognize that all things are within their power to control and that love brings harmony to all things. It becomes their choice to move into the power of love.

Judgments are the basis of third-dimensional reality. Eartheans compare their truth to everyone else's. They compare their illusion to everyone else's. They feel pride, goodness, emotional love, hate, anger, frustration, and all of the other emotions because of their reactions to these judgments.

As volunteers and the Eartheans move into the fourth dimension, they realize that judgments do not serve them. They begin the process of impersonal living. They begin to observe the process of life without the need to judge or evaluate others. They become aware that they are, indeed, producing their own play, and everybody else is producing and living in their own plays. They recognize that because they are so busy with *their* play, they couldn't possibly know all of the details of someone else's. So they accept this lack of information and do not attempt to judge or direct others. Thus, much of the need for judgment simply falls away. (*This freedom from judgment is vital to move into fifth-dimensional reality.*)

In the fourth dimension, the concept of God expands. No longer is God someone who punishes or rewards. Instead, the God Essence expands until it cannot be contained within the confines of the old image of God, and Eartheans then realize that the God Essence is a part of all and all are part of the God Essence.

In the fourth dimension, Eartheans begin to incorporate unconditional love and acceptance into their lives. They begin to realize that only through unconditional love can they fully attain their Earthean power.

Fifth Dimension

The fifth dimension requires total surrender to the God Essence or soul/spirit. Which one of these the Eartheans choose is not important, for the spirit/self is directly connected to the God Source. The act of surrender to Divine will is significant, for it represents relinquishing control to the forces of unconditional love or higher consciousness. Through this process, Eartheans learn to harmonize their individual frequency with the vibrations of the higher forces.

The fifth dimension brings unconditional love and acceptance into the Earthean daily life. They experience the unity with the God Essence. This dimensional reality does not accept the concept of a punishing, demanding, or rewarding God. Eartheans existing in the fifth dimension would never humble themselves before God, because they recognize, in their new understanding, that God would not find that behavior acceptable. The fifth-dimensional God Essence is a force that unifies and binds all things together. This God would want humanity to come with heads held high to accept the gifts of abundance from a loving God who is gender-free. This God would never want or expect subservience or perfection in the Earthean form from His/Her/Its children. Rather, God would want someone with a loving and pure heart, who wishes to continue to grow and ascend to higher and higher levels.

In the fifth dimension, Eartheans recognize they are not separate from the God Essence but are part of the great whole. *All are one* in the fifth-dimensional reality.

The God Essence is seen as the great Creator who endowed humanity with the ability to co-create. A fifth-dimensional person would never violate this great gift. Volunteers recognize that they do not have to create with the mind or use visualization to create. Instead, they begin to understand that their creative nature continually creates with every thought, word, and deed.

Volunteers in the fifth-dimensional consciousness experience the truth that *all are one*. There is no separation. All pain is their pain; all hurt is their hurt; and what happens to that little puppy on the street also happens to them. They know that all things impact them and they impact all things. Fifth-dimensional Eartheans know compassion as few others can.

Many fifth-dimensional children who feel the pain of others experience well-meaning, third-dimensional adults telling them they are silly. These children feel a powerful connection to all, so it is hard for them to understand how adults can pass by without noticing, feeling, or caring.

All conscious separation ends in the fifth dimension. Groups come together for the greater good. Competition is replaced with co-operation, which creates group harmony. These groups focus on the common good and build on common ground. In the third dimension, group members see differences. In the fifth, commonality is seen.

Relationships are very important in the fifth dimension. Relations are neither personal nor emotional, but transpersonal/impersonal. Eartheans acknowledge their relationship with all living things—the animal, plant, and mineral kingdoms, the Earth, the moon, the air, the oceans, the universe, to name just a few. Native Americans understood and lived this relationship to the fullest.

Eartheans recognize, at this fifth-dimensional level, the existence of the extraterrestrials, so contact and involvement with brothers and sisters of space take on new expression. Eartheans know, *and know they know*, that this existence is not just this plane, this physical space, this planet, but is made up of many universes and types of existences.

Thus, Eartheans learn that there are beings who work for the good of the planet and others who work for its control and domination. It is not judged nor embraced, only acknowledged as expressions of the realities of others. It is at this dimensional reality that Eartheans often learn of their true nature, and many recognize that they are, indeed, volunteers. It is at this frequency that the conscious mind allows access to the greater wisdom, which contains an awareness of off-planet activity, other lifetimes in service, and other planetary experiences.

It is at this point where many volunteers move into their total personal power and commitment to the greater service or shy away from active duty because they fear losing their sanity or their ability to do all that they came to do.

Making the transition to fifth dimension can be smooth and without difficulty, or it can be just the opposite. But you may not have a choice about making the change. Because the collective, dimensional consciousness on the Earth is affected by the individual frequencies of the volunteers, it is continually being raised. Eartheans will either resist the frequency, causing themselves great discomfort, or they will accept this greater reality, making the transition much easier.

Sixth Dimension

As the vibrational frequency ascends to the sixth dimension, meaning is found in sounds, symbols, and tones. Language becomes less and less important. Eartheans begin to recognize the wasted energy that words represent. Words become less and less capable of expressing Earthean knowing, for there are no words to express these new insights and truths. These are signals of the journey into the sixth dimension.

In each higher dimension, the former reality becomes more unreal. All beliefs are laid open for examination and reexamination. Old issues must be processed anew and brought to closure. Those issues that were repressed in lower dimensions rise to the surface until they are dealt with and resolved.

As volunteers move into the sixth-dimensional level, they begin to understand why they had to break up old beliefs and why they were unable to use language to express their reality. They know such volumes in a flash, that it would take hours to convert it to words, if, indeed, it were even possible to find words to convey the meaning. A sixth-dimensional being has great difficulty explaining to a third-dimensional person what this dimension is because it is beyond language.

It is similar to what happens when you dream and have kaleidoscopic experiences that weave in and out. The dream made sense as it was dreamed, but trying to explain it to someone else is impossible.

At the sixth-dimensional level exists a reality of symbolism. There are colors and light and music and exquisite beauty. It is beyond what can be fathomed in third dimension and, thus, hard to describe. It is a level of perception beyond the reality of physical existence.

When volunteers are exposed to sixth-dimensional frequencies, they assist others to move more quickly out of third dimension into fourth, or out of fourth into fifth.

Mother Earth is not yet ready for such a pure sixth-dimensional frequency, but sixth-dimensional frequencies will help accelerate the planet into the fifth dimension. This is the reason why many volunteers are drawn to symbols, mantras, tones, and pictographic-type symbols. If properly used, these can assist Eartheans to awaken to higher realities. *Volunteers are warned, however, not to become dependent on any form, symbol, or tone outside of themselves. The power is within, never without.* These items are tools that can help, but never substitute for, conscious, directed thought at the higher frequencies.

Mathematics originated in the sixth dimension. When you truly understand the principles behind mathematics, you are in touch with very great forces. Many people perceive Einstein and others of his intellectual equal as being able to go beyond physical reality, and they were. That is why he and others broke from the traditional view of reality and talked of things not normally thought about. These people were not born greater than any other, but they tuned in and thereby became great. Eartheans who reach this level usually choose to disassociate themselves from many normal human activities, for those activities, to them, no longer serve any purpose. In the sixth dimension they work solely for the good of all; the individual is of little significance.

In a sixth-dimensional reality, the physical body loses its significance; therefore, for the most part, it does not play a part in the Earthean growth experience because it is not an important part of reality. Eartheans who achieve the highest sixth-dimensional frequency may appear or disappear at will. They have mastered the limitation of physical existence. It is the highest level in which a physical form is used.

Seventh Dimension

In the seventh dimension, there are no physical bodies, for the need for physical confinement no longer exists. There are no further lessons to learn from the body; therefore, it is left behind. However, you do have a unique, seventh-dimensional form. Perhaps it would be a pure spirit form or light body or perhaps an expression of color, sound, or tone. The individuality of the entity still exists, but much like a drop in the ocean. Beings exist in the totality of creation, but are aware of the unique droplet they are.

In this dimensional consciousness, one learns lessons of unique expression outside the limitations of physical form. It is a state of connection with Divine Source beyond the limits of language. One knows all because of the quality and clarity of one's connection with All-That-Is.

Eighth Dimension

Beyond the seventh dimension, there is only the universal, the collective, the mass. There is no longer specific, individual process or form. One feels the unity because they *are* the unity. Beings exist in the ebb and tide of universal flow. At this level, there is no separateness between one drop in the ocean and the ocean.

Eighth dimension is void because no form exists or is needed. The sound of the universe rings constantly (though felt, not heard). It is similar to that heard in a large seashell. Beings experience the flow of the universe in this dimension. All are a part of All-That-Is, but it is recognized that there are still new experiences in consciousness.

All consciousness swirls like ocean tides. No separation exists, yet beings are aware of their influencing presence. Just as a committee is formed on the Earth plane to define larger purposes, so, too, do individuals willingly give up individuality to experience collective awareness.

From the eighth dimension, group consciousness exists as a single manifestation. Perhaps like a group of friends who are very, very close and who decide to unite for a common purpose, these collective, eighth-dimensional consciousnesses literally become one essence that contains the attributes of all the entities involved.

Eighth-dimensional reality is a kind of marriage of spirits. The marriage can work in many ways, including choosing a physical form ambassador on Earth for this eighth-dimensional group consciousness. Nothing is lost, but only combined; the group synergy creates a much vaster reality. As one moves up through the frequency dimensions, the element of separation that is so important a factor in third- and fourth-dimensional life, is gradually eliminated by the increasing awareness that separation itself is the illusion upon which the lower frequencies are based. Purification of the individual becomes much more important, until, at this level, the individual is no longer necessary.

The method whereby increasing unity occurs is the unifying of collective groups with larger and larger groups. Oftentimes, when communicating with other dimensions, those communications refer to themselves as "we" when asked, "Who is there?" The we represents a much larger unit consciousness.

These consciousness units continue to grow until they represent hundreds of thousands of combined individual souls/spirits. This is but a phase of preparation as one moves up the dimensions. The ultimate purpose is unification with the God Consciousness in a totality of perception. Individuals' energies see the need to come together, feeling increasingly comfortable with losing their individual identity (seventh dimension) and combining with like consciousnesses, to create a greater whole.

Many lessons are learned in each dimension, but it is the eighth dimension which prepares the way for total unification with All-That-Is. As a group consciousness moves beyond the need for lessons and growth at this level, it moves into ninth-dimensional consciousness.

Ninth Dimension

In the ninth dimension, group consciousnesses choose to come together en masse to manifest as planets, galaxies, stars, or universes, and they create a much greater collective reality. They create an environment in which masses of other beings continue their growth.

They combined in the eighth dimension, but in the ninth these combinations grow exponentially, putting themselves in service for the greater good. They see the importance of the greater reality, so they offer themselves as an opportunity for growth to others. This is the ultimate experience of unconditional love and unselfish service.

At the third-dimensional level, Eartheans may help others because they feel the need to fix or heal them. In fourth-dimensional reality, individuals offer aid or help only when asked. At the fifth dimension, one feels little need to interfere with the life experiences of others because one recognizes the growth opportunities they contain. No interference of any kind in the life or affairs of another would occur in the seventh or eighth dimensions. In ninth dimensional reality, one gives oneself totally into service for the growth opportunities of others because there is no perceived difference between self and "others."

Never is growth forced upon another; new opportunities are offered to those who wish to continue their growth. With the present Earthean concept of time and space, it is difficult to conceive that Mother Earth is simply such a unit of consciousness. She is a beloved ninth-dimensional being who has given freely of herself in order to provide growth opportunities for those who choose to experience her uniqueness.

Let us use the metaphor of a child who grows to adulthood, learning lessons along the way. The adult chooses to create a child and continues to grow by experiencing the growth of the child. Thus do ninth-dimensional beings grow through the experience of others. Ninth-dimensional beings are often identified by the honored title of Mother.

The growth opportunities afforded by a ninth dimensional consciousness can also be related to a laboratory learning environment. The researchers learn by providing an environment in which others experience and grow. Thus, Mother Earth learns by experiencing the growth and behavior of those in residence.

Each ninth-dimensional consciousness offers new opportunities. When Mother Earth moved into existence, her gift was the gift of free will. On this planet, alone in all of the universes and universes beyond universes, beings had the opportunity to experience the manifestation of their free will choice. Therefore, planet Earth offers a diversity of form found nowhere else.

Physical density was one choice offered on Earth, but it was not required. Only when the vibrational frequency became so low that it could not support the free moving in and out of physical matter, were Eartheans trapped by their choices. But this was, indeed, free will in action. On Earth, free will is the Divine plan. And this was good, as the Divine plan always is.

Unfortunately, for humanity, these extremely low vibrational frequencies were never expected to be the Earthean choices; therefore Mother Earth was not prepared for them. It is these extremely low frequencies that jeopardize the continued existence of beloved Mother Earth. It is these extremely low-frequency consequences of Eartheans' choices which brought the Earth-based volunteers to this planet. It is these extremely low frequencies which make the changes on this planet necessary.

The change being birthed on Mother Earth now is the dimensional shift from third-dimensional to a fifth-dimensional reality; a shift from duality and separateness to one of unity and love.

The shift will occur. The Earth-based volunteers are here to act as midwives to the process. This can be a painless and relatively simple birth or one that requires much time and causes much agony. *Choosing is how free will teaches us, and all on planet Earth will help decide. The more love, peace, and unity are chosen, the greater ease of transition will occur on this planet.*

In the end, the change will occur just the same. Beloved Mother Earth, who suffers so much now because of the vibrational choices of humanity, awaits patiently for the outcome.

Each thought, word, and deed chosen by every person living on Earth determines how long and how severe the labor pains. Choose now to choose love, peace, unity, forgiveness, and compassion, and in that choice, Mother Earth is healed. This is the true mission of each Earth-based volunteer and each light worker in all the universe.

A Message from Mother Earth to the
Many Earth-Based Volunteers

I feel the love that many of you send daily, and it acts like a tonic to my system. You, in turn, feel my pain and suffering and it causes you great concern. Trust that we are connected by choice and that when you help yourself, you also help me, for you have agreed to carry my burden. You have agreed to release me from the bondage of these lower frequencies.

Do not judge another's perceptions or life experiences, as this causes you, too, to incur these lower frequencies. Because we are connected, I am again affected.

Learn to trust your own source of greatness. Learn to allow the greater wisdom, which is a part of your own source of power, to guide your way. Trust your heart and soul to provide all that you need in this physical density.

The way is not easy, but you did not expect it to be so when you volunteered. Do all that you do in a light-filled and loving way, and your Earthean assignment can be shortened.

Lie on your belly and listen to my heart and feel my pulse. This will renew your sense of purpose and re-membrance of the Earthean mission, as some of you have lost your bearings. As you do this, ask All-That-Is

*to send love through you and into my beingness. I need
this and so do you.*

*You do not need to burn down the buildings of those
who pollute my water, as this causes more hate and fear
and only serves to further my pain. They do not mean
to destroy my existence. They operate out of fear...fear
of lack.*

*Teach all by example, how to bring in the light, and
live in the love vibration. Teach all how to move beyond fear and judgment. Teach all how to manifest all
they need.*

*I will teach you all that you need to know, for this is
my true nature. It is the reason for my existence. I
want you to have all.*

*You do not need to hoard my life blood, which you call
water. Ask me and I can give you all the clean, spar-
kling drink you want. You do not need to drain my lu-
bricant to oil your motors. This makes my existence
more uncomfortable, much like your dry skin. Ask me
and I will give you unlimited free power and technol-
ogy. To receive all that you need and desire, you must
first move into a state of responsibility for all. You must
first remember your Source, from which all choice comes.*

*I am ready and so are you. I have existed long enough
with Eartheans' state of anger and fear. My vibrations*

have been held too low for too long through forces of
destruction. Too many wars have been fought for silly
reasons that have no meaning in the greater reality.
Lift up thine eyes and see the light. The wisdom awaits
you. I await you. Awaken to All-That-Is. Awaken to all
that you are.

Mother Earth could choose death, for she, too, has choice. Death is simply a transformation from one form to another, even for a planet. If she were to give up her physical form, she would be free to choose another ninth-dimensional existence. Or if she felt herself ready, she could move into a higher state of reality.

But she chooses this not. She wishes to continue to allow Eartheans to learn in this reality. Therefore she fights for her very life, for if she were to die, no other planet could or would replace her. The lessons learned on Earth would simply not be available for others.

There are three dimensions beyond the ninth dimension, but as far as the volunteers are concerned, they are not important at this time (except to say that tenth dimensional beings help create ninth dimensional environments—thus, many who helped with the forming of this planet are now in Earthean form as volunteers to help rescue her). For most Eartheans, these dimensions are beyond their comprehension. Far more important is to realize the great healing power of unconditional love and make this vibrational frequency the basis of all that occurs in physical life.

The volunteers have an important role to play on this beloved planet. It is time to awaken. This, too, is the Divine plan and this is good, as the Divine plan always is.

Chapter Thirteen

Directions for Awakening

Many years ago it was said that for every thousand people who come to the Earth with a mission, only one will awaken to that mission; and for every thousand light workers who awaken to their mission, only one will have the courage and faith to carry out that mission. The following suggestions are given to help volunteers both to awaken to their Divine mission and develop the courage to fulfill it. I trust they will be helpful.

The directions for awakening are clear and can be used by all people of all ages. These steps will awaken humanity to its greatest good as well as the greater good of Mother Earth. They will reunite humans with their heavenly Father/Mother/God and His/Her/Its loving vibration. They will also awaken the Earth-based volunteers to their pre-arranged mission on Earth.

Talk to the Heavenly God Source

Take time to talk to the God Source, for all is heard. This can be accomplished in the form of conversation as you drive or go about your daily routine or through a more formal prayer. The choice matters not, for either way you are recognizing and acknowledging the God Force's presence in your life. You are calling in that vibration. You are bridging the Divine frequency with your thoughts. This will have a positive effect on your own vibrational frequency. With each communication, either formal or informal, the relationship is strengthened.

Ask for Help

Remember that God, or any of the Divine servants, can do nothing *unless you request help*, for free will is the Divine law. They would never intervene without a request. Ask for help, ask to be shown the way, ask for clarification of your purpose, ask for *"this or something better, for my highest and best good and the highest and best good of all concerned."* By using this phrase when you ask for something, you are recognizing that there is a higher view than your Earthly eyes allow. You are giving those who have a better vantage point an opportunity to work on your behalf. You are allowing the God Essence and the heavenly guardians to assist you while you are in the physical.

When the time comes that you feel you are ready to surrender personal will to Divine will, know that you must surrender 100% to really be of use. God needs to work through many helpers on beloved Mother Earth to achieve the desired end. Each becomes the right hand of God, allowing the God Source to work through him/her and help anchor heaven to Earth. Reciting the Lord's Prayer with Divine intent assists with this process.

Give Thanks

Give thanks, for prayers are always answered. An attitude of gratitude assists you in opening to a greater world of abundance. *Know that whatever comes into your life is for your best and highest good.*

Always look for the good and the needed lesson in every situation, no matter what it looks like or how painful the experience. Recognize the lessons in the lives of others. Do not judge either your or their experiences. Simply accept the lessons, and as you raise your vibrational frequency, you will no longer have need of many of them. Know that you may be choosing to experience something unpleasant so that you may help someone else later on.

Learn to Exist in Your State of Center

Centering yourself is the art of utilizing your physical energy so it is in harmony with your spiritual energy. It is the process of connecting the physical you with the God Source. It can best be compared to driving a car with manual transmission and changing gears.

Imagine driving your car in first gear all the time. Think how the engine would struggle to keep up the speed and of the added stress that this inappropriate gear would cause the engine. There is nothing wrong with first gear; it is appropriate for low speeds. But when you get up to 10-15 miles per hour, you had better know how to shift, if you want to take care of your car.

When your engine gets to these higher speeds, it's time to shift. People accustomed to driving a manual transmission don't need to look at the speedometer. They know, through their familiarity with the sound of the engine, when it is time to shift. They become attuned to it and respond to its unspoken needs. Each engine is different, requiring shifting at slightly different times, so each driver must listen and respond accordingly. Now it's time to become familiar with your physical body and its engine.

Centering is the process of shifting gears in your physical body. Most people have been running their engines at a relatively slow speed—a first gear of sorts. It may not feel like you have been going slow, but, in the cosmic sense, you have. Because of the speeding up of time and the other subtle Earth energy shifts, most people are now feeling the need to shift to a higher, more comfortable gear. Centering is the process of doing just that. The process of physically shifting gears is like the car engine that speeds up when the gears are shifted but sounds slower. The faster you go in your center (the higher your frequency), the more still you become, much like the gyroscope in the center of an ocean liner stabilizes it in the face of buffeting waves. You become immersed in the stillness and the internal place of peace. It is the place where "the joy that passes understanding" can be found.

Next time you are feeling stressed, take a moment to focus your attention on how you are feeling physically. Pay attention to your heart, lungs, emotional well-being, and your mind. This will help you know what your body feels like when it needs centering. More than likely, even though you are used to this physical condition, you are racing your engine and it desperately needs to be shifted.

Instructions for centering are simple and straight forward. Just do it. Move to your center. It can appear in your imagination like a beach, a woods, or even a void. You can say the words, "I move to my center and place of power." You can think the thoughts or just know that you have done it. All techniques are equally powerful, for *it is your intent that makes it happen.*

Feel your feelings now. For an added boost, take three deep breaths, each time focusing on breathing in Divine will, universal harmony, and/or Christ light. You may use any image or word that you desire, for all of these things are of the same source. Consciously breathe out anything that does not serve you. After the three breaths, stop and again sense how you feel. This is what you feel like when you are in Divine harmony. As you do this more often, you will begin to sense when you are out of connection; thus, you can learn to recognize when you need to shift. Eventually, the time will come when you are always in your place of center and Divine connection.

Take Time to Listen

Take time to listen to the wee, small voice. This can be as simple as lying in the bathtub, clearing your mind, and allowing your consciousness to float along. Be ever receptive to thoughts that float into conscious awareness.

Meditation, which is a more formal form of *listening*, may also be used. Meditation has many forms; it matters not which you use. Anything that permits you to still your mind for at least three minutes will serve this purpose. Have no expectations. Listen with your heart, soul and inner guidance. You may gradually feel the need for longer periods of silence.

Do not become concerned because you have friends that see vivid images during their meditations and you see nothing. Remember that each person has different needs and has developed different skills over many lifetimes. Trust that you have what you need and they have what they need. If your quiet time allows you to feel less stressed and more at peace within yourself, the meditation has served its intended purpose.

Nor should you become concerned if you drift off to sleep during times of stillness. It may be that your conscious mind feels you are not ready for conscious awareness, thus blocking your awareness. It cannot, however, block the experience. Trust that it is happening for your best interest.

Still the Conscious Mind

A mind out of control is like carrying around a backseat driver. You can be talking to a friend and the mind chatters, "Look at that! Do you believe that hair? Boy, she looks old...Wonder if she's back with her husband..." In this situation, the mind actually separates you from the experience. Another place where you may notice the runaway mind is at the theater. You are trying to enjoy the movie, but it chatters, "That actress could do a better job... Did you see that?... Wasn't that fake-looking?... That was dangerous..." If it were someone sitting next to you, you wouldn't hesitate to tell them to be quiet, but you allow your mind to ramble without limits.

Yes, it is possible to still the mind. Use the steps listed above. You will feel the difference. You will be able to experience life and people without all the distractions. By bringing your mind into balance, you will find that it will become more available to assist when needed but not so invasive in your experiences.

If you have difficulty stilling the mind, talk to it lovingly but firmly, as a loving parent would talk to a disobedient child. Tell it why it is important for it to be still and why this is in the best interests of all. If this does not work for you, ask for help. The mind has been given the job of guardian to the gates of knowing. This powerful position determines what is known and not known at the conscious level. This power can be intoxicating and hard to relinquish. The mind may not readily and willingly give up this powerful position. You have free will and the right to choose, so persist, if it is for your highest good.

Follow Your Inner Guidance

Follow your inner guidance. Trust your intuition. Ask for discernment in your everyday life. Allow truth to enter your consciousness. *Do the thing that you know to do.* Take action if action is called for or requested. Rest if you feel the need to rest. Eat, sleep, work, and play based on the dictates of your inner voice, not by established routines or the desires of others. As you make a commitment to God to cooperate with Divine will, be receptive to directions. If your heart is sincere, the directions will come. Then, your level of trust will help you to follow the directions given.

Maintain Integrity in All You Do

Now is the time to maintain personal and professional integrity in everything you do. Integrity has been defined as having your belief and value structure in agreement with or in harmony with your behavior. Now is the time to walk your talk and talk your walk. *Over the next few years, everything out of integrity will fail.*

If you say you follow your inner guidance, yet you do not follow that wee, small, voice because you are afraid of what others will say, then you are out of integrity. If you admit to having difficulty following inner guidance and then don't follow it, then you are in integrity.

If you believe you are living in the vibration of unconditional love but allow all sorts of Earthean conflicts to disturb you, you are out of integrity; whereas, if you recognize the conflicts as lessons in letting go and don't allow these challenges to disturb your inner harmony, then you are in integrity.

If you say or believe you are an honest person, but freely alter the truth to fit your needs, you are out of integrity. If you know and admit to yourself that you say what needs to be said to fit your purpose, then you are in integrity.

If you feel angry toward someone and yet pretend to be loving toward them, you are out of integrity; whereas, if you recognize and honor your angry feelings and deal with them (which does not imply taking action toward the other person, but just being honest in your dealings with them), you are in integrity.

If you do not feel like giving someone a hug, yet do it anyway, you are out of integrity. If you do not feel like giving someone a hug and own and respect your feelings, you are in integrity.

If you say yes when you want to say no, you are out of integrity. If you go along with something you know is not right, you are out of integrity. If you confront it and/or refuse to be a part of it then, you are in integrity.

Integrity is a very important part of the new day on Terra. All must move into integrity to carry the highest vibration. Integrity does not imply that you must be perfect or above reproach, but it does mean that you must be responsible for every thought, word, and deed and always be in harmony with your beliefs. The art of "talking out of both sides of your mouth" will no longer be acceptable.

Maintain the Vibration of Universal Love

Maintain the love vibration at all times. At first this will be very difficult. Do your best and ask for help. Gradually you will be able to stay in the love mode for longer and longer periods of time. When you fail to feel love, investigate to find out why. These can be important lessons for your own growth. Periodically stop and ask the angels, higher self, or friends from other dimensions to fill your totality with love. As you feel these wonderful sensations (for they *always* respond), give thanks and act in a way that maintains these feelings. This is somewhat like walking while balancing a book on your head. It is difficult at first because it causes you to concentrate on the act of walking. It becomes easier with practice.

You must allow the love essence to come through you at all times. *Your inner being is all love essence.* The physical body tries to contain the love, but it must not be contained. It is to be broadcast to the wind, Earth, and every energy form it contacts. Love spreads and grows the more it is allowed freedom of expression. You must never try to hold it back. Eartheans have held back the love essence much too much already.

**Free Yourself From Any Vibrational Frequency
Which Serves You Not**

There are many forces, both intentional and accidental, that serve to prevent you from moving into your highest frequency and your place of power. Becoming aware of how you feel when these lower vibrational forces are influencing you is the first step in freeing yourself from their bondage.

A simple prayer or affirmation can do the trick. Use this one as a sample. It will do the job for you. Feel free to alter it in any way that feels comfortable.

I am a child of the universe. As such, I am worthy, I deserve good, and I call to me all that is for my highest and best good and the highest and best good for all concerned. Protect me from all that dims my light or slows my steps. Let me be influenced only by those things that will further my growth and assist me to know truth.

If I have allowed anything or anyone that no longer serves me to influence me, I demand that I be released from that influence and that it or they never again be allowed to bother me. I surround them with love and send them to their highest good, as I do with anything or anyone that tries to slow my progress or interferes with my Earthean experience. So be it! It is done!

There is a power in three, so I recommend repeating this three times. You are welcome to begin this prayer/affirmation with a *Dear God* and end with an *Amen*, if you like. It matters not, as God hears all your thoughts and words anyway. Also, you may want to say it every morning and evening until its truth is your truth. You will feel how long it takes.

Accept the Reality Behind the Illusion

Accept the reality behind the illusion. When your life is closing in on you, remind yourself that this is all a game designed to help you grow. Stop and determine why you would have brought this to yourself (for truly you did). Ask yourself, *"What am I trying to learn from this experience, person, or event?"* Send love to the situation or person who is triggering unpleasant reactions in your life. These things have come into your life as a guest, by your invitation. These invitations usually are not made on a conscious level, but the law of free will dictates that these situations could not affect you without your consent.

Know that every strong emotional reaction illuminates a lesson in your life and is an opportunity for growth. People around you love you enough to reflect that which you will not examine in your own life. They are neither positive nor negative. If the attribute you react to were not present in your own being, it would go unrecognized in someone else. Therefore, it is important to notice your reactions to others. Which of your personal attributes appear to stand out the most in others? What lesson do they contain?

Help Others Only When Help Is Requested

Help others only when they request your assistance. Know that others, too, are on a personal journey, and although you may think you know what is best for them, truly you do not. By the same token, those of the highest realms are bound by these same laws. They may help you only if you ask, so do not hesitate to ask when help is needed. Do not limit your asking to your physical friends; ask the universe, for there are many friends in different dimensions who are willing to help.

Do all that you can to meet your own earthly challenges, as this causes growth. When needed, ask and allow others to serve you and assist you through your challenges, as this assists them with their own growth. Service is a large part of the Earth lesson and by serving others and allowing others to serve you, you actually assist the healing of the vibrational frequency on this planet. Just as you have chosen your mission, so they, too, have chosen theirs.

Trust All-That-Is

Trust All-That-Is. Trust your own wisdom. Trust the wisdom of Divine will. *If you feel you made a less-than-best choice, simply choose to choose again.* Do not beat up yourself because you fail to live up to your own unrealistic expectations. Perfection exists only in the movies. It is the content of your heart that is the most important. Do not concern yourself with the thoughts of others, for they, too, are operating in the physical and, thus, have limited vision. Instead, concern yourself with the God Force's loving purpose for you. *Remember, you are to be a model with your life. You are to be a beacon of light for Eartheans to use for their highest good.* You are not to judge their use of this light. You are NOT to judge. *Every judgment will take you farther away from God's will.*

Release Fear and Judgment

Learn to recognize fear and judgment as downward vibrational adjustments. Then simply choose not to have them. If you do feel the feelings associated with fear and judgment, allow them, and then move beyond them. *Fear lowers your frequency and judgment alters it. Both serve no one and cause great damage to the person and beloved Mother Earth.* Fear and judgment keep humans from moving into their full power. Fear and judgment put Eartheans in a vibrational state which makes them open to control. Choose to release fear and judgment from your vibrational field.

When you feel fear's paralyzing effect on your energy system, do whatever you can do to get your energy moving again. Sing, dance, move, or pray. All these will get your energy going, which dispels fear and its effects. Trust that what you do is right for you. You can always ask the angels for help; they do love to be of assistance!

If you catch yourself moving into judgment (especially against self), then choose to choose again. Release the judgment with love. See it as a thought form moving into the light, where it is transformed to a thing of beauty. You may also feel the need to pray/affirm:

> *I am a child of God and as such I am perfect. I accept who I am and what I am in this moment. I am open to change as I learn the lessons life offers me. I am aware that if I knew everything about everything and had reached a state of perfect perfection, I would have no need of the lessons Earth offers. I accept who I am fully and trust that I do my best in all situations. I am always open to growth and know that every day, in every way, I am getting better and better. I accept and honor myself and all that I am.*

> *So, too, do I recognize that all on Earth are doing the best they can. They, too, are here for growth, and therefore I move from judgment of others into total acceptance. I honor their path. The Infinite Intelligence created diversity on Mother Earth, and therefore I recognize the wisdom of diversity. I accept that there is no one right way but a variety of ways to learn. Some may choose*

pain and suffering, whereas others choose a softer, gentler way. I look at the paths of others only so that I may be better aware of how I can serve humanity and Mother Earth.

I am what I am and I allow all that I can be to take expression. So be it! It is done!

Honor and Respect All Paths and All Life Forms

All creation is holy and a part of the God Source; therefore, to show dishonor to any one of them is to bring dishonor to the God Source. Native Americans chose to walk in harmony with all creation. We are fast approaching a time when this must be done again. To walk in disharmony with totality is to self-destruct.

We are moving into a vibrational pattern that will not allow any form of disrespect to be shown to another. No longer will we be able to deny the personal power and influence of women or ethnic and religious minorities. No person will be able to increase his/her power by suppressing another's. All people will be honored regardless of age, weight, sexual orientation, or planet of origin. Plants, animals, and minerals will be honored for their role on this planet. All must be recognized and respected for their great gifts.

Build Constructive and Productive Thought Bridges

The Earth-based volunteers must now become fully aware of and responsible for all of their thoughts. This is a time when all Eartheans' energy is speeding up, and this is causing thoughts to become more powerful. Thoughts are a basic form of creation and carry great influence on this planet. To think is to create.

To think on someone or something is to build an energy bridge to that person, place, or event. A bridge allows energy flow in both directions. If you open yourself, via your thoughts, to a lesser light, you allow that lesser energy into your existence. If you flood that being with light and love and then close the bridge, you have allowed your energy to impact theirs without allowing them to influence you. If you read, watch, and think about tragedy, you allow that vibrational reality into your life. If you read, watch, and think about love, peace, harmony, the God Source, and so on, you allow that vibrational reality into your life.

With each thought you have, you are both sending and receiving a vibrational energy that may or may not serve you. *Each thought is a choice.* You are responsible for all thoughts, whether they are intentional or not.

One technique for truly becoming responsible is to speak aloud all your thoughts. This requires much courage and commitment, but it does make you fully aware of your thoughts. The time is quickly approaching where all will know your thoughts through your energy patterns. There will be no deception on Earth, as your intentions in all situations will be fully obvious. Prepare now.

Laugh at Life

Laugh at life. Life is a grand game designed by a loving and giving Creator/Source. The God Essence gives you whatever you want for playing this Earthean game. Therefore, it is your responsibility to ask for all that is good and helpful for you and your fellow Eartheans.

Laughter helps to change your perspective of life. It loosens the self-forged chains in which humanity has wrapped itself. You serve humanity well when you can inspire laughter. Do not take life, yourself, or God's mission for you too seriously.

Keep Your Life in Balance

There is sometimes a tendency to run off to a mountain peak or a solitary cave to continue your spiritual growth. Your progress will have the most impact if you keep your life in balance. You need to learn to harmonize your physical, mental, and spiritual growth.

You have a physical body that eats, sleeps, feels emotions, cleans the floors, and senses the Earthly world of illusion through manifested thought. None of these are good or bad; they simply are. Experience them but do not become entrapped by them. Feel the pleasure and the comfort; allow yourself to experience the abundance that life has to offer. Physical existence was never meant to be a life of hardship and lack. Pamper your body. Balance play with work, leisure with effort, and learn to appreciate each aspect for its unique contribution to your growth.

You have a mental mind that enjoys thinking, reasoning, learning, and growing. Use it. Turn your heavy-duty problems over to your mind before retiring to bed. Review the details and outline the problem. Let your mind work on the problem as you sleep. Upon arising, or when you least expect it, the solution will pop out of thin air. Thank your mind and show your appreciation, for this is the purpose for which it was intended.

Your spiritual growth also needs to be a part of a balanced life. The Earth-based volunteers came to be part of the Earth experience; therefore, no matter how advanced you become, you are still expected to be a normal person. You may still need to keep your job, wash your dishes, take out the trash, and other such mundane tasks.

You may feel the need to read, meditate, sing, take classes, or pray all day. Remember that for all things there is a season. Keep your life in balance. Excess in any one area may slow your progress more than help it. You may feel the urge to go and preach to the world; this, too, may be counterproductive. Your loving, balanced life will be the model that most helps the world, and the world begins with your children, family, neighbors, and co-workers. Share your love, and the rest will take care of itself. You will serve your spiritual growth and your God Essence best by learning to love unconditionally. This, of course, comes from listening to your inner guidance.

Do not be surprised by a shifting of your priorities. The important things of yesterday may not be the important things of tomorrow. You will feel a shift from outer reality to inner reality. You may find the goals you made for yourself last week no longer important today. Relax and go with the flow in the new direction.

Remember Your Source

Finally, as you drift off to sleep, remember who you really are—a child of the God Source, a spark of the pure God Essence. See yourself as the light of the Radiant One. Visualize yourself as a being of light. See yourself removing the crusty layers you have wrapped yourself in for so many years. Feel the vibrations shift as you hold this thought.

Awaken to all that you are and all that you can be. Awaken to your Divinity and mission. Mother Earth needs you.

So be it.

There are many excellent books, tapes, and people who have much to offer. Those that are of the Highest Source remind you that the only way to reach your full potential is to

GO WITHIN
GO WITHIN
GO WITHIN
GO WITHIN

GO WITHIN

GO WITHIN

GO WITHIN

GO WITHIN

GO WITHIN

A Word About the Author,
Dr. Heather Anne Harder

Dr. Heather Anne Harder's experience with children, and those they interact with, spans the past 23 years. She has been a public school teacher, a reading specialist, founder and director of four child-care centers, and has taught at the university level for over 14 years. Most recently she was a professor of education at Governor's State University, University Park, IL., where she coordinated both the graduate and undergraduate early childhood program.

Dr. Harder was awarded bachelor and master of science degrees in elementary education from Indiana University and a doctoral degree from Indiana State University.

Recently she has chosen to resign from the university in order to work full time for the universe. "Working for the universe," she says, "has long hours but great benefits."

Dr. Harder lives "peacefully" with her two daughters and husband. Kerri, age 20, and Stacie, age 16, and Bob have provided much growth and many lessons along her Earthean path. They continue to be a source of joy in her everyday life.

She had always been an avid reader and enjoyed reading anything and everything concerning the world of the paranormal. She believed that "weird stuff" did happen, but there had not been room for it in her fact-filled life. She had been raised and trained to study, research, and rely on proof to formulate her mindset.

Several years ago she began to have interesting experiences which changed all that. Her spiritual awakening had begun and so had her inward adventure. Until that time she had a fulfilling but comparatively uneventful life. During her time of awakening, doors and windows began to open and new vistas were glimpsed. Her world would never again be the same.

During her entire adult life, she had chosen not to read works of fiction because she did not want to clutter her mind with other people's imagination. (The story of her spiritual awakening is told more fully in her book, *Exploring Life's Last Frontier: The World of Death, Dying and Letting Go.*) Now, she will tell you, her life story reads more like a work of fiction than a real-life adventure. She currently operates successfully in two worlds, one she labels her third-dimensional, "normal" world and the other she respectfully labels "weird and wonderful."

To date, she has authored numerous articles and three books, *Many Were Called—Few Were Chosen: The Story of Mother Earth and the Earth-Based Volunteers; Perfect Power in Consciousness;* and *Exploring Life's Last Frontier: The World of Death, Dying and Letting Go.* All contain perspectives and universal truths, as seen through her human eyes at their time of creation.

Heather maintains a busy speaking schedule. She travels both nationally and internationally, sharing her truth and love. Her insights are always offered with light and laughter, which others are free to accept or reject at their discretion. She honors all paths to enlightenment and recognizes the wisdom of diversity.

She is the founder of The Association of Universal Light Volunteers (AULV) and commits much of her time to personal and planetary healing and growth.

You may call Light Publishing or the AULV office to receive a schedule of her travel plans, to be placed on the mailing list, or to make arrangements for her to speak in your area.

A Letter From Heather

Dear Friends,

This book tells the story of Mother Earth and how we all became a part of her experience. The Divine Plan for Mother Earth is free will. But there are many forces now in place that wish to limit humanity's free will. By inducing fear and judgment, our free will is selectively limited. By passing laws which prohibit many options while determining few opportunities, our leaders are again systematically reducing free will.

Our forefathers, who were, indeed, Earth-based volunteers, had great foresight when they designed a constitution which limited the power of a central government and guaranteed basic rights for all citizens. Now, both our rights and our responsibilities are being destroyed, as we move ever closer to a controlled society, thus violating the heart of the Divine Plan. Because we have chosen to live on Earth at this time, we are entitled to impact what happens on this planet.

I feel strongly that the Earth-based volunteers must become involved again with the direction of our government and limit the powers of our leaders. They have stepped outside the boundary of what is right and just. Control and manipulation are destructive forces and must be eliminated from the hearts of humanity and from the powers of our leadership.

You can help by praying that God's will prevail on this planet. Prayer is the strongest force throughout the universe, and when enough people unite in prayer, the change will be complete. I strongly suggest that no specific action or behavior be requested, but to pray only for God's will to manifest on Earth. The Lord's Prayer says it very nicely: "...Thy Kingdom come. Thy will be done, on Earth as it is in Heaven."

There are great forces in place which alienate one form of religion against another. These same forces are attempting to remove all forms of spiritual beliefs from all public offices, schools, and places. There have even been attempts to take any form of religious symbols from all work places. If you choose to wear a Christian cross or a Star of David as a pin, then your employer could be sued. These are feeble attempts to distort or sever humanity's awareness of its Divine Connection. A world that has been created to ensure diversity in all things does not exist to hold a single ideology or thought. All connections with God are equally sacred and are, thus, equally honored. All names for the God source are equally held reverent. We must unite in prayer to ensure that all rights of belief are protected.

I am a member of a family of six children. Each of us children had a unique relationship to our physical Mother and Father. All were equally special, yet quite different. Would our relationship with our Spiritual Father/Mother/God be different? All volunteers search for that Divine connection and recognize it when it is found. Each will achieve it by following a different path. All paths are perfect in the Creator's eyes.

Now is the time to stop judging the rightness of the paths of others and join together in a single purpose to bring about heaven on earth through love, unity, and service. Anything which blocks this action must be confronted with love and not allowed to exist. Physical force is not the way, but by utilizing the power of love and prayer, all things are possible. Where light is, darkness cannot exist. The light workers, or Earthean volunteers, are being asked to bring the light and love to this planet. They are being asked to give up the ways of the old in order to herald in the ways of the new.

A new day is dawning on Mother Earth, and we are here to share in the wondrous moment. But as the old saying goes, "It is always darkest before the dawn," and we will have to experience the darkest hour. *The days, months, and years ahead will be the most challenging that this planet has ever seen.* We are here to comfort Mother Earth and humanity. We are here to bring a joy to this transition.

We can and we will succeed. We are on the side of God, and God is always victorious. The feeble attempts at control and manipulation by a few will only bring disastrous results to them. They are not the ones we need to focus upon. Rather, we must keep our eyes on the beauty of Mother Earth and place our faith in Divine Will.

Until now, volunteers have led individual lives, with little awareness of their part in the greater picture, but that is slowly changing. *The time is near for us to understand the big picture.* The Bible talks about a time when the soul shall be restored. To me, this means a time when all shall be made known. Specifically, the soul's path, both past and present, will become whole and complete and no mystery will remain.

That time is now. We will come together will others of like mind to do our Heavenly Creator's business. Our skin color, hair, religious beliefs, standard of living, and body parts may be different, but our hearts will beat as one. We are coming together to serve the greater good. We are coming together to heal a planet torn apart by hate, violence, fear, and judgments. We are coming together to anchor the heavenly energy of unconditional love to our beloved Mother Earth.

When we have completed this process, we will live in a very different world. Some parts of this planet may be physically very different. Areas that cannot be healed may have to be plowed under, much like a farmer would plow under a field to enrich the life force in it. This will happen to ensure the survival of the planet. Our reactions to these changes will determine how much and how long the transition process will last. Love and prayer can speed the process as well as lessen the severity of the experience.

Old beliefs and attitudes must be allowed to flow and change according to God's plan. Our prayers to know truth and do God's Will will become more powerful as we open to trust.

We must trust the Divine wisdom that is orchestrating the happenings. We must follow our own inner guidance, which guides our lives. We must pray that Divine will be done.

When the process is complete and Earth is in her full glory, all the Earth-based volunteers can step back in pride and say, "...and I helped!" For surely we have played a part in this great time. I am told that then we will have a thousand year vacation. Earth will continue on her evolutionary path primarily without volunteer assistance, until a time when we return for one more rescue mission. Then our commitment will be complete. For those of you who may be moaning, know that it is always a choice, and you are never forced to do anything, especially return to Earth.

As for me, I am being asked to step forward into a place of great challenge. I will be tested in all areas, both personally and spiritually. As you read the next few pages, know that they come from a place of great sincerity. If you feel led to assist in any way, I look forward to hearing from you. The Earthean path is not always easy, but it is always followed by great reward. Pray for me as I pray for you and Beloved Mother Earth.

Much Light and Love,

Heather

A Campaign for the Presidency

Dr. Heather Anne Harder has chosen to assist this country achieve its "Perfect Power in Consciousness" by seeking the Presidential nomination for 1996.

Governmental experience is teaching us that the ways of the past are not working in today's world. It is time for a loving transformation.

As a woman, her presence in the Oval Office alone will create a totally new atmosphere. The fact that she has never participated in the political field means she owes no one any "favors" and she cannot perpetuate a faulty system.

Dr. Harder, as a university professor, has shown her ability to ignite the spark of learning and fan its flames to produce a glowing light of knowledge. Her academic experience has also served to teach her the value of guidance from those who are experts in their fields. That guidance will play an important part in her efforts to bring about the changes needed to recapture the true essence of a government for the people and by the people.

Dr. Harder has no illusions about the strenuous path she has undertaken, which is why she has begun her campaign early. Unlike those who work within the system, she has chosen to take her campaign directly to the people, just as she plans to do as President.

- If you are interested in having Dr. Harder speak in front of your organization to share her views and answer questions concerning her campaign for the office of President, contact either Deborah McGrew, at (219) 662-7074, or Adrianne Bacavis, at (219) 663-5011.

- While Dr. Harder is trimming away as much as possible of the unneeded expense involved in campaigning for President, funds are still a necessary part of the process. If you feel so inclined, any contribution may be sent to: The Committee to Elect Dr. Heather Anne Harder President, 210 So. Main St., Suite 102, Crown Point, IN 46307.

- For those wish to support Dr. Harder in the campaign process, there are a multitude of ways to assist. For further information, contact Deborah McGrew, at (219) 662-7074, or Adrianne Bacavis, at (219) 663-5011.

Dr. *Heather Anne* HARDER

PRESIDENT '96
"A New Vision for a Changing World"

210 S. Main Street, Suite 102
Crown Point, IN 46307
Phone: (219) 663-7340
FAX: (219) 663-9974

Dear Friend and Concerned Citizen,

Are you tired of politicians promising change but delivering more of the same? Are you tired of a government that is so complicated that you need years of training to understand it? Are you tired of feeling that *your* government no longer cares how you feel about the issues? Do you really want four more years of government-as-usual, or are you ready for a real change in leadership?

Four years ago I reached the point when I had had enough. I decided that if, indeed, real change was to come to our government, there would have to be more personal involvement on my part. It was at this point that I made the decision to run for the office of President of the United States of America in 1996. I fully understand there is a very small chance of my winning, and I am aware of the very large cost, both financially and emotionally. However, I feel if I don't get involved now, then my dissatisfaction is merely lip service, as I watch this country move toward a point of no return. It is time for all of us to stand up and make our government listen. After all, we are the bosses of our elected officials. We must lead the way.

"Who am I?" you might ask. I am Dr. Heather Anne Harder, and I would like to become the next President of this great nation. First, let me tell you what I am not. I am not a politician. I am not rich. I am not crazy. Now, let me tell you what I am. I am a forty-six year old American woman who is a wife, mother, businesswoman, and author. My background is in education, and I pride myself on my ability to deal with people on many levels concerning our most precious resources, children and families. As a speaker and consultant to organizations, businesses, and schools, I have traveled extensively. Combined with prior experience as a university professor, I see myself as having moved from local educator to global instructor.

In many respects I am very ordinary, except that I have extraordinary courage. I am willing to enter the political arena to do my best to make a difference in the way our country is run. I am willing to risk my comfortable lifestyle for public scrutiny in order to do this.

My greatest preparation for this massive job is that I have lived a very normal life, with no political experience. Therefore, I have not been tainted by the current system. Having never been a politician, I cannot perpetuate a faltering system, and I owe no political favors. I do not claim to have all the answers that will solve this nation's ills, but I am able to draw upon my ability to seek, heed, and assimilate counsel from the wisest and most qualified. My desire is to simplify and reduce the existing federal bureaucracy to something the average American can understand.

My intentions as President of the United States, and as such, a major influence in the operation of this country, are:

1. To return the federal government to its original intent, as documented in the Constitution, thereby giving power and responsibility back to the people of the state, where it was designed to be.

2. To expose secrets that are destroying the fiber of our government. I am told that there is classified information above the level of the President. If this is true, who makes that decision? ... And why? A government with no secrets is more truly a nation that is "by the people and for the people." Collectively, WE are the people, and it is time to reclaim OUR power from the clutches of those with a personal agenda. To demonstrate my earnest desire to eliminate secrets, I am publishing a book which exposes all my personal secrets. I am not looking forward to its release, but I know a President must lead by example.

3. To support a government "of the people and BY THE PEOPLE!" Through technological achievement, today's world enables our country to become a "true" democracy within the Republic through the institution of FEDERAL REFERENDUMS. This method of "direct input" allows you to have a real and direct impact on your government. You would speak directly, and be heard, on very important and/or controversial issues.

4. To make vote fraud an act of treason. With so much information surfacing about the electronic manipulation of our polls, it is time we sent a strong message, to those who would choose to alter the will of the people, that this will not be tolerated.

If this is beginning to sound like something you find interesting, then get involved with the political system and do something now. The majority of Americans today choose to stay out of politics because they feel it is too _____ (dirty, ugly, corrupt, non-responsive, etc. ... Choose your own word). That excuse is no longer valid. Hundreds of thousands of people went along with Hitler during World War II and, in hindsight, we can see the destruction that caused. It is time to stand up and say, "ENOUGH!" and then ask yourself, "What can I do to help?" You can start by praying daily for this country and following the dictates of your heart.

This is probably the first campaign "chain letter" you've ever seen. It is a creative alternative to our extremely expensive campaigning traditions. According to some experts, it costs approximately $25 million to run a Presidential primary campaign. I am about $25 million short! I need your help. Please sign the bottom of the following campaign letter and add a personal note, if you feel so inclined. Make copies and send them to your friends and relatives. Consider sending them to those on your holiday card list. (You can also call Campaign Headquarters (219) 663-7340 to receive bulk copies, if you prefer.) Sending the letter does not necessarily mean that you support me personally. It does mean that you agree that the need for real change is here, and you want those you care about to know that I exist. Then keep the chain going. Let people know that in 1996 there will be a *real alternative*.

In the past, chain letters have promised participants everything from perfect health to vast amounts of money if they continue the chain. The only promise I make is that by continuing the letter, you will become part of a great force that can bring about needed change in our government. If you break this chain, no curses will befall you. However, you will increase the chance of more government-as-usual. Furthermore, you will increase the likelihood that another professional, plastic politician gets into office. This country deserves better ... YOU deserve better! Now is the time to make copies, sign the bottom, and send them on their way.

Much Light and Love,

Dr. Heather Anne Harder and Friends

If you would like to help...

☑ Check me out. Call or write Campaign Headquarters for more information. I will be happy to supply you with literature on the issues of your choice.

☑ Tell your friends about me. Name recognition is very important. If nothing else, I have lots of courage, as did our forefathers who founded this great nation. They, too, had little experience in designing a country, but they took action because they knew change was needed.

☑ Write letters of endorsement. These can be personal or organizational. Please send copies to Campaign Headquarters. Remember to target Democratic leaders, local newspapers, and elected officials.

☑ Become involved. Many volunteers are needed to win in 1996. Send for the booklet, "101 Ways to Support Dr. Heather Anne Harder for President." Join the "Club of 10's." If you have skills or expertise that would be useful to the campaign, I especially need YOU.

☑ Give a donation to the cost of campaigning. Any amount from $1 to $1,000 will help and is much appreciated. (According to federal mandate, an individual's contribution cannot exceed $1,000; however, businesses and PACs may give more. Call for details.)

☑ Contact organizations, clubs, bookstores, and other groups to schedule a live presentation. Call Campaign Headquarters to see when I'm available. Call (219) 663-7340 or write to The Committee to Elect Dr. Heather Anne Harder President, 210 So. Main St., Suite 102, Crown Point, IN 46307.

☑ Pray for this country and its leaders, and for guidance. Then do ALL you feel guided to do. Prayers ARE answered and our country needs YOUR help.

Introducing...

The Association of Universal Light Volunteers (AULV)

My spirit friends stated that it is now time for humanity to step forward and publicly claim their Light volunteer status. Therefore, The Association of Universal Light Volunteers (AULV) has been founded.

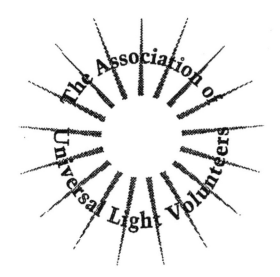

The AULV Mission Statement and Affirmation

We, who gather in the glow of universal love, offer our services to all who seek them, in whatever way we can assist and whenever called upon to do so.

The AULV Purpose

1. To provide a forum to publicly acclaim one's intention of dedicating one's life energy for the well-being of Mother Earth, humanity, universal peace, and harmony.

2. To provide a professional organization for light volunteers who endeavor on behalf of universal love and light.

3. To share growth experiences and offer light to others of like mind and purpose along the spiritual path of life.

4. To respect and honor the diversity represented on this planet and recognize the infinite wisdom which created diversity within all things.

5. To recognize and honor the oneness of all.

6. To promote a better understanding among all people and to find the common ground in all physical, mental, emotional, and spiritual areas. No single ideology or "right" behavior is dictated by the organization. All who serve the Light walk a Divine Path.

7. To publish and disseminate (in a timely manner) universal truths, as needed, to bring about personal and universal harmony.

8. To provide a network to offer unselfish service for all those who seek to know truth and receive universal guidance, at no cost.

9. To provide, at the least possible cost, opportunities for spiritual seekers to experience, first hand, the energies of sacred sites around the world.

Corporate/Business Memberships

Corporate/business memberships are available for a $100 donation for those who wish to dedicate their business to serving the Light. With or without the donation, AULV's hope is that you make a public affirmation (silently or aloud) that you dedicate your business to bettering humanity and offer your business to serve the Light. When you affirm, either silently or verbally, this empowers those of the highest Light to work through you and your business for the highest good of all.

All corporate and business memberships will be listed as sponsors on all AULV special events and conferences.

AULV MEMBERSHIP FORM

_____

Name (Please Print)

_____

Address

_____

City   State   Zip

_____

Daytime Phone   Evening Phone

MEMBERSHIP AGREEMENT

I am a light worker, a child of God, known by many names, who has come to Earth to bring peace and love to a troubled planet. In physical form I do not have to be perfect; I only have to do my best and do it with unconditional love. I have read and do acknowledge the organization's mission statement and will repeat it frequently in order to remind myself of my Divine purpose here on Earth.

I am enclosing my $5.00* membership fee. This covers the cost of processing my membership, my quarterly subscription to _Light Reading_, and my membership pin. These are to remind me of the Divine Light which I represent here on Earth.

_____

Signature   Date

* You are welcome to decrease or increase your membership fee, based on your financial situation. Membership money will be used to support the mission of the organization. All services are offered via unconditional love to all who indicate a need.

Return this membership application (or a photocopy) to:

AULV
210 So. Main St., Suite 202
Crown Point, IN 46307

For more information, call the AULV office at: **(219) 662-7074.**

BOOKS BY DR. HEATHER ANNE HARDER

Many Were Called—Few Were Chosen: The Story of Mother Earth and the Earth-Based Volunteers. This is the awesome story of Mother Earth, from her perfect beginning to her threatened existence today, and of the Earth-based volunteers who've answered the call to aid her. It describes humanity's evolvement from freedom to bondage, the destructive effect of our free will choices upon Mother Earth, and the Divine Plan for the ascension of Mother Earth and all who are willing to ascend with her. $13.95, soft cover.

Perfect Power in Consciousness describes the preparation needed to achieve inner harmony and spiritual ascension. It outlines the physical, spiritual, and mental alterations that occur during this process, both on a personal and a planetary level. The reader will discover that all experiences are opportunities to learn and grow in the school of life. $12.95, soft cover.

Exploring Life's Last Frontier: The World of Death, Dying and Letting Go. *Leading Edge Review* described this book by saying, "Heather Anne Harder, Ph.D., divides her inspiring new book into three sections. First, she establishes her credibility; then she shares some of her experiences with the dimension beyond life; and lastly, she discusses the process of transition into the next world and provides a technique to penetrate the limits of life while you are alive. A must for anyone exploring the limits of life." $15.95, soft cover.

These books can be purchased from your local bookstore or you may order them directly from Light Publishing. Please add 15% for shipping and handling ($2.50 minimum). Send your check or money order to:

LIGHT PUBLISHING

Light Publishing
210 So. Main St., Suite 203
Crown Point, IN 46307

or call (219) 662-7248 for further information.